LIVING
WITH
TELEVISION

LIVING
WITH
TELEVISION

Ira Glick
& Sidney J. Levy

Preface by W. Lloyd Warner
With a new introduction by Kurt Lang

Routledge
Taylor & Francis Group

LONDON AND NEW YORK

First published 1962 by Transaction Publishers

Published 2017 by Routledge
2 Park Square, Milton Park, Abingdon, Oxon OX14 4RN
711 Third Avenue, New York, NY 10017, USA

Routledge is an imprint of the Taylor & Francis Group, an informa business

Library of Congress Catalog Number: 2005052022

Library of Congress Cataloging-in-Publication Data

Glick, Ira O. (Ira Oscar), 1927-
    Living with television / Ira Glick and Sidney J. Levy ; preface by W.
Lloyd Warner ; with a new introduction by Kurt Lang.
        p. cm
        Originally published: Chicago, Aldine Pub. Co., 1962, in series: Social
research studies in contemporary life.
        Includes bibliographical references and index.
        ISBN 0-202-30796-4 (alk. paper)
        1. Television broadcasting. 2. Television viewers—Attitudes. I. Levy,
Sidney J., 1921- II. Title.

PN1992.5.G55   2005
302.23'45—dc22   2005052022

ISBN 13: 978-0-202-30796-1 (pbk)

TABLE OF CONTENTS

INTRODUCTION TO THE
ALDINETRANSACTION EDITION

Based on studies conducted between 1957 and 1961, this book recalls what life in America was like before the television set in the living room became a family fixture. It should serve as a period piece for that dwindling number of us old enough to remember this decade, evoking memories of by-gone attitudes toward television and the programs people once viewed and talked about. It should make all of us—however young—aware of the many ways in which not only television but research about television have changed since the days when both were still in their infancy. Not only were screens far smaller than today but, for most people, color was still around the corner. Most households could afford only one set, which made viewing very much a family affair, with the set occupying a prominent place in the living room and parents and children often watching together. The highly popular programs they jointly enjoyed, such as *Gunsmoke*, *Father Knows Best*, *Ozzie and Harriet*, *The Price is Right*, and the names of TV personalities whom they allowed to enter their lives, among them Red Skelton, Garry Moore, Tennessee Ernie Ford, Fred MacMurray, are no longer widely familiar. Some have been practically erased from the histori-cal memory. Or, to switch perspective from the past to the future: how many television viewers, producers, program directors, and researchers in 1960 could have anticipated how much the largely self-imposed content restrictions, then in effect, would erode? Back then, characters in sitcoms did not casually commit marital infidelity, contemplate abortion, or utter now acceptable expletives. On the other hand, cigarette advertising, once the mainstay of popular shows, has been largely banished to be replaced, in part, by the repeat appearances of a former U.S. senator and Republican presidential candidate as the pitchman for a pharmaceutical to cure erectile dysfunction, not to mention public discussion of condom use to prevent the spread of AIDS.

These are not surface changes. They reflect the competition among the three networks that dominated the airwaves, each vying for a larger share of the "great audience," a term popularized by Gilbert Seldes, a now forgotten pundit of the popular arts. The large amount of free time people spent watching the limited number of programs translated into remarkably high program ratings. Not that viewers were undiscriminating. Their viewing choices were based on information available to them about both the humans and the fictional characters they met on the screen, many of whom they came to consider personal acquaintances who became a vital part of their everyday world. Indeed, many programs were "real" for those who loyally followed their personal dramas. There was no need then for networks to boost ratings by offering what are currently labeled"reality" shows. This sense of having been put in touch with "reality" through exposure to televised shows extended also to newscasts. Television, it was widely believed, allowed people to "see for themselves" and, even though, over the years, trust in television news has declined, faith in the impressions conveyed "through one's own eyes" seems somehow to have survived.

Meanwhile, the additional television channels made possible, first by the expansion of the spectrum and then by cable and satellite dishes, have created an abundance of program material. These technologies have chipped away at the conceptualization of the television audience as a "mass audience," appropriate at a time when pay programs for television-on-demand were still in their experimental stage and the video-recording devices that enabled home viewers to save programs for later watching (with unwanted commercials edited out) were not yet available for either love or money. With the home computer fast becoming a household staple, technology has allowed advertisers to create and disseminate individually focused ads that pop up in response to keyword searches on search engines like Google or Yahoo. Finally, as television goes digital, televiewers should be able to download just about anything from the airwaves for their personal use. All these things have been undermining the economic structure of television broadcasting as described in this book.

Research methods have also reaped the benefits of advances in recording and transmission technologies. These same video-recorders and computers give researchers the tools to replay any program or commercial in its original version or to edit it so as to serve a variety of objectives. Data collected in experiments or on-line surveys can then be fed directly into computers able to handle previously unimaginable amounts of data, tabulate them almost instantaneously, and perform complex statistical analysis. Aided by rapidly advancing technology, researchers have managed to fine tune their messages by locating vulnerabilities of potential recipients and to tease out effects that eluded predecessors whose methodological efforts, judging by current standards, might seem to be rather unsophisticated.

Given these methodological advances some readers may be tempted to downgrade *Living with Television* as not especially "scientific." I would strongly disagree. It certainly reflects careful interpretation of data collected by methods that were then state of the art and in some places are still employed today. There is a heavy reliance on the large number of fully open-ended questions collected in sixty-nine surveys, for which a total of 13,479 persons were interviewed, the large majority by telephone. Contact by phone is still the accepted method despite the increasing number of people who own only cell phones and the increasing use of online surveys. The investigators followed time-honored procedures in asking respondents how often they watched, what they liked or disliked, what they remembered, and in confronting them with paired word choices from which they were to select the one that better fit the program. But they do something more than tabulate for their commercial sponsors such phenomena as how much time Americans in different social categories were spending on watching television, audience size as it varied by time of day, season, number of stations in a market, special programming pr for the ratings and demographics of individual programs. Nor will those interested in the effect on ratings of such factors as place on the program schedule and competition in the same time segment find it here. More than likely, data of this genre were contained in reports to the commercial sponsor who funded these surveys but, to put it bluntly, this book contains no statistics, not even purely descriptive ones, beyond the two tables on the demographics of the samples for the different inquiries and on the total number of people interviewed—information that, quite appropriately, is relegated to an appendix on methods.

This volume draws on the large number of fully open-ended questions from these same interviews, questions that, instead of being standardized, were revised and sharpened on the basis of insights gained. To call this approach qualitative, as opposed to quantitative, hardly does the book justice. Focus groups, currently in wide use, are also qualitative but typically serve to zero in and put into sharp focus how and to what participants will respond positively or negatively. The view on the television landscape here offered is more panoramic with details filled in as they let their camera roam from place to place. The method and mode of presentation exemplify the social anthropological approach of W. Lloyd Warner, the co-founder with Burleigh Gardner of Social Science, Inc., the commercial firm that conducted these studies for a company interested in maximizing the advertising potential of television. Warner, who contributed an introduction to the original volume, had made a name for himself with observations of the multi-layered culture of "Yankee City," a New England town, whose class structure he delineated in terms of the different networks in which people participated and the values and prevalent lifestyles associated with each. Once so well known was Warner for his classification that those who read a best-selling novel by John P. Marquand had no trouble in recognizing him as the model for his fictional anthropologist.

Indeed, Social Research, Inc. was an unusual firm. For at least a while it retained a close connection to the University of Chicago, where Warner and Gardner had both been on the faculty and where they continued to attract graduate students to that institution. Both Glick and Levy completed their doctoral work there—Glick in sociology and Levy in the interdisciplinary program called human development. All adhered to a tradition which stressed the need to "understand" human relationships in their full complexity, a tradition they carried into their commercial work, using their "background of trying to understand the dynamics of behavior and attitude and then, *if appropriate* [italics mine], to quantify them." Gardner, in reminiscing about this period, further notes that in the age of computers, "it is easy to be entranced by the beauties of statistical differences and the masses of quantitative output and to lose sight of the need to understand what is going on." Of course, these researchers also made use of multivariate analysis of quantitative data but gave equal amount of attention to responses to open-ended questions and projective tests

without reducing them to abstract statistics. Instead, they relied on their interpretative skills as social scientists to explain
how different kinds of people actually functioned. Their reports to clients were "discursive, telling what we have
learned...."[1]

Still, one cannot avoid asking how much of these findings
about the uses of television still applies. The introduction of
new communication technologies always has consequences.
Television, when it arrived, unsettled some habits long established. Its most immediate effect was on disposable leisure time. As video took over from radio, listening to once
popular entertainment shows declined sharply; movie attendance decreased, and so did socializing outside the home.
Readership of the more specialized magazines pretty much
held its own. At first people watched almost everything but,
once the novelty wore off, the amount of time so spent, as
recorded in surveys of time budgets, maintained a consistently high plateau that lasted for decades but with remarkably small displacements of other leisure activities. People
managed to maintain this time usage pattern, partly because
of shorter work weeks but also because they learned to crowd
more and more activities into the same time slot. More of the
television viewing took place while people were also doing
something else.[2]

Viewing habits also adapted to the increased range of
choices made possible by technological advances noted. To
underline this point: cable subscribers now have access to
nearly a hundred channels whereas in earlier years they were
lucky to enjoy good reception on three to seven stations. The
resultant abundance of television choices proved a boon not
only for commercial stations targeting a niche audience but
also for government agencies and nonprofit organizations
intent on reaching a particular constituency. Such endeavors
gained viability as households with multiple sets became the
norm for the middle-class family. As a result, the television

audience is more segmented, that is less of a mass audience than it was half-a-century before. Furthermore, to the extent that every member of a household now has his or her own set, the prototypical American image, so prominent in the 1950s, of a family—of two parents and their children (possibly with a dog)—grouped around the set forfeits some of its validity. Family viewing, if it occurs at all, is less likely to involve a regularly scheduled favorite TV show than a video rented from one of the stores found in every neighborhood.

Computers linked to the worldwide web caused a further quantum jump in the range of viewing choice, not only in the availability of entertainment but even more of all sorts of information, practical advice, and even moral guidance. An Internet connection puts computer users who are able to navigate this universe in a unique position. They can freely search for whatever satisfies their most idiosyncratic tastes. To be sure, as of now, only a minority of Americans go online regularly but the number is fast growing. Before very long, most of us will be able to download just about anything—from current musical hits to the kind of performances for which most people still look to television. Computer connection will also enable people to take courses, participate in discussion, and make their voices heard. How this will affect their once-intimate relationship to television remains open to speculation. Preliminary information shows that Internet users spend significantly less time watching television than non-users and, when they do watch, a proportionately greater amount is as a secondary activity.[3] The relationship between computer use and television is complex, partly because access to the necessary technology is still beyond the means of many households and, more tellingly, because the frequency with which any individual will abandon television for the Internet not only varies according to a person's distinctive circumstances but is also affected by what each medium has to offer.

Important as technology may be in determining the part television will play in people's lives, attitudes toward the medium are at least equally determining. This is the theme that resonates throughout this book. Bringing some order into this variety, Glick and Levy distinguish among three attitudes toward television: The largest numbers of viewers, at least during these early years, *embraced* television. Their attitude implied "a strong and general acceptance of television, its abundant use, great familiarity, considerable enjoyment, and a profound gratitude for its presence and availability" (p. 46). For these viewers television was first and foremost a source of entertainment. They felt an intimate bond to the medium that left them unconcerned over the possibly deleterious cognitive and behavioral effects of "too much" viewing. Nor did they ever voice any fear that the sexual allusions or frequent violence on some programs could undermine moral standards among the young. But—and this is an important caveat— very few among this mass of viewers were found to fit the stereotype, held by many critics then and now, of high TV use as an addiction, something viewers so afflicted cannot shake or are prone to use as an escape from problems too overwhelming to be faced directly. Quite the contrary. These viewers knew what they liked, were well informed, and judged programs by their own standards. High television use is not entirely without intellectual stimulation.

The other end in the attitudinal continuum set forth by the authors is occupied by persons more critical of television, which they see as providing programs harmful to children, containing too much "immorality, sex" (even then!), of swallowing up time usefully spent in other activities, of excessive commercialism and potentially misleading ads. Such a litany of criticisms, though still voiced today, was not widely shared. Glick and Levy found that it came mostly from upper-middle-class people, intellectuals, and professional social critics prone to vocalize any discomfort with television, which explains the frequency with this theme entered the public discourse. Persons with an attitude toward the medium expressed as *protest* also engaged in the least casual viewing and made some effort to control the programs their children watched. For them, turning on their TV set, was much more an act of conscious choice than part of a daily routine. But practice and attitude do not fully coincide. Protesters, according to Glick and Levy, "do not differ in their pattern of watching from those who view it [television] in a more receptive way.... Protest and criticism often come as hindsight, more as a matter of guilt over having slipped, having lost self-discipline, than of actually avoiding the set in the first place" (p. 77). This impression has been confirmed in strictly quantitative surveys of attitudes. Respondents who told interviewers that there was "not enough" information and "not enough" food for thought on television, though somewhat more likely to select more serious programming, often bypassed such opportunities. Despite their demands that television provide more enlightenment, these same people" select[ed] it only one fifth of the time that they [were] watching while it [was] actually available."[4] That actual behavior does not fully accord with expressed attitude does not prove these persons hypocrites. Rather, it describes how television even intrudes into the lives of people with great reservations.

So deeply has this intrusion spread that all but a handful of purists who reject everything about the medium have had to cope with its ubiquitous presence. Glick and Levy see the future dominated by people with an *accommodating* attitude, one that lies between a full embrace of the medium and the critical views of protesters. Their attitude leaves ample room for a full enjoyment of televised entertainment but with some remaining concern about the time it absorbs. This ambivalence toward the medium makes these accommodators rather self-conscious in deciding what they should watch. It goes with demands for programs of high quality and efforts to keep themselves informed and to discipline themselves not to view too much. Using their sets "in the same free-and-easy, taken-for-granted, unplanned way" of embracers is simply inconsistent with their attitude (p. 98). Although accommodators comprised less than a plurality of the television audience in its early years, the authors saw their type of usage gaining ground as people grew more comfortable with television, became better able to select the programs that best met their own interests, and learned to integrate the time spent watching television with others activities that give them satisfaction. This prediction seems borne out by previously mentioned time budget studies.

Protest, on the other hand, has not disappeared but rather shifted away from its originally upper-middle-class base. The loudest clamor in recent years has emanated from spokesmen for conservative Christians. The concerns they voice are less a reflection of a general attitude toward television than aversion to specific content, mostly of an explicitly sexual nature, including public service ads for hygienic practices such as condom use. One of the more contentious incidents that stirred up a minor storm was the flap at the 2004 football Super Bowl when, due to a so-called "wardrobe malfunction," the singing star Janet Jackson "accidentally" showed a bare breast. Had the half-time extravaganza in which Jackson was taking part been televised late at night or on a niche channel, it would at most have raised a few eyebrows among those just chancing to tune in. But having been telecast in prime time to a mass audience that included millions of nonadults, its airing was entirely unacceptable to the protesters whose loud voices are most often heard today.

A problem with this typology, ranging as it does along a continuum with one attitude or pattern shading into the next, is the lack of criteria for drawing boundaries. Here the typology, as in so many other cases, functions only as a heuristic device, used skillfully by the authors as a peg on which to hang their thick description of variegated television use. They offer little by way of explanation beyond their resort to the elementary social categories of social class, age, sex, and family role (particularly in relation to child-rearing), categories seen as associated with differences in the life-style with which attitudes toward television are congruent. The two-dimensional chart they draw of gender and class is a simple one. It helps us see relationships with an undeniable face validity, such as the proposition that television holds an extra attraction for people who are homebound—young children as well as the sick, the frail, and the aged. The characterization of teenagers, making the transition from dependency on parents to forming their own adult identities, as predominantly protesters is a bit more shaky, even though most of them, uniformly across class lines, tend to prefer viewing with their own age group to viewing television in the family room. But to class them with the protesters, as they are in the schema, strikes me as stretching the definition. What remains of their "protest" when programs are clearly targeted toward this age group and they have a place to watch them either alone or with their own chosen friends? The social class model applies most clearly to adults in households containing children, whatever their ages, with protesters concentrated in the upper middle class, accommodation more typically a lower-middle-lass syndrome, and the embracing attitude most typical of people who fit Warner's upper lower class, that is, people of limited income trying to maintain their respectability.

No single research strategy can provide all the answers. The authors are forthright in their acknowledgment that these schematic representations catch no more than the most general attitudes. The real value of this book lies in the vignettes drawn from extended quotes indicative of how respondents deal with and feel about television. These accounts breathe life into the schema as does an equally extensive discussion of each program type and its appeal. Although program preferences differ by gender and social class with each category having a distinct set of favorites, there is also a good deal of audience overlap. For example, the program category called "comedians" is depicted as favored by just about everyone. Here again the schematic presentation blurs the distinctions within the category. Comedians do not all appeal to the same audience. Each one appeals to the extent that persona and personal style match the preferences of some segment, large or small, of the potential audience for television.

This last observation deserves to be expanded because implicit in it is a lesson. It holds that the "audience" as much as the content of communication is a determinant of the response. One does not have to follow Roland Barthes all the way to his dethroning of the author to recognize that different viewers look for different things and that their orientations, beyond affecting what they choose to view, significantly affect what they get out of any program. Sometimes their responses may contradict those intended by producers. Thus, a weekly sitcom, conceived as pure entertainment and not to be taken too seriously, serves some viewers as an invitation to develop a psychological relationship to one or more of its main characters while still others look to it for moral guidance or practical advice. Informational programs also grant viewers some leeway. The claims of news producers to legitimacy rest on the assumption that the audiences for political campaigns seek guidance in deciding how to vote when, in fact, many of them follow the coverage much as they would a sports event, looking for excitement, or to demonstrate loyalty to a candidate during a hard-fought contest. In this "game,' performance can be as important as substance, with the participants in a political debate, for instance, judged by their ability to deliver a knockout blow or by the skill with which they dissimulate.

In closing let me emphasize that Glick and Levy's conclusions, based on data from studies commissioned by a commercial firm, are in one sense somewhat restricted but in another sense broader than one might expect. They are broader—to say it once again—in exploring the full range of meanings viewers extracted from television programs against the background of American culture as it existed in the 1950s. The designers of these studies obviously persuaded the sponsor that their findings would be of use to commercial firms searching for an audience receptive to their commercials. At the same time they are restricted insofar as the authors in their presentation of these findings never quite rise above the level of description. As a result, some of what they have to say may appear dated since television and the modes of viewing have changed, especially to a generation for whom W. Lloyd Warner has ceased to be a household name. But readers should recognize that the authors regard viewing and program choice as a reflection of an underlying ethos, something Bourdieu has since called *habitus*. Beyond that, as is also true of Pierre Bourdieu's work, the old concepts of class culture have limited explanatory value. In this respect, the authentic depictions of how people have dealt with the flood of images that threaten to overwhelm them mark no more than a first step, albeit an important one, along a long road others should be eager to follow. Therein lies the real value of what I have called a period piece.

Kurt Lang

Notes

1. Burleigh B. Gardner, Doing Business with Management. Applied Anthropology in America, Elizabeth M. Eddy & William L., Partridge (eds.). New York: Columbia University Press, 1978, p. 256.
2. For some relevant data, see John P. Robinson and Geoffrey Godbey, Time for Life: How Americans Use their Time. University Park: Pennsylvania State University Press, 1997.
3. Barry Wellman and Caroline Haythornthwaite, The Internet in Everyday Life. London: Blackwell, 2002.
4. Gary A. Steiner, The People Look at Television: A Study of Audience Attitudes. New York: Alfred A. Knopf, 1963, 188.

PREFACE

From its beginning, television in America has been a fighting word, a battleground, a stormy topic filled with many conflicts. When it began, upper-middle-class people, always the self-anointed guardians of the public taste, morality, and right thinking, scornfully treated it as beneath their attention; yet their many words about it were shrill with interest and concern. The campus intellectuals, particularly the bicycle set, made not owning an "idiot box" a significant sign of their intellectual superiority. The motion-picture people feared and fought it, the TV patent owners struggled viciously among themselves. Meanwhile, the increasingly affluent families of the common man, particularly the working classes, purchased TV sets by the million, and in little more than a decade, most American homes had one or more sets. The motion pictures, at first warily, sold reruns; later, they sold large schedules of their better pictures, and soon they were producing their own TV shows. Upper-middle-class children soon crossed the "TV line" and invaded their neighbors' houses to see Hopalong Cassidy, and sometimes their mamas went with them to look at Peter Pan. Then the professors at the universities and their more lofty graduate students warmed themselves before the intellectual image of Adlai or the protectiveness of Ike, often sneaking in an illicit view of some of the more popular programs.

TV soon had won all its battles. America from coast to coast had become a TV nation. Yet, the fighting—as a matter of fact, ten dozen fights—continues bigger than ever. Everyone now has his own opinions about violence, sex, boredom, lack of good judgment and taste in the selection of programs; in general, all the ideas everyone has about everything are re-expressed in terms of the adequacies or inadequacies of TV programs and their commercials. Discussion about TV is still highly emotional. The questions asked about it and the assumptions made are loaded and are stated in controversial language. Only recently have there been efforts to find out what TV is, as a growing cultural reality and a way of acting in which 180 million Americans are involved.

A very few studies have tried to find out objectively what TV is, as a social and psychological phenomenon, and to discuss its function and significance to its many audiences. Among these few, the present volume ranks high as a contribution to our understanding of this extraordinary phenomenon. Its lucid writing and attractive style, freed from the jargon of the behaviorial sciences, give the reader a calm, objective picture of what TV is today and what it is in process of becoming. At the same time, *Living with Television* is an exciting contribution to our body of knowledge about the meanings and functions of the symbol systems commonly shared by most Americans.

To understand the meanings and functions of television in America, the authors have examined the programs presented on TV by conducting many field researches that extended through several years. They have viewed these programs as meaningful objects that arouse the feelings and mental concerns of the viewers. In addition, with the use of appropriate social and psychological techniques, they have interviewed those who did and did not listen to the many varieties of programs commonly presented on national television, to find out how various audiences responded. They have carefully identified and classified members of the various audiences by such necessary categories as age, sex, social class, and many other important social characteristics. For deeper and more fundamental insight, they have used depth interviews and similar procedures to learn the meaning and significance of various programs and their symbols at the less conscious psychological levels. In brief, by relating audiences and their responses to the characters, activities, and plots of the many programs studied, they have been able to arrive at a series of interpretations and generalizations about an important segment of the symbolic life of Americans and to report on the meanings and functions that these symbols have for many varieties of our countrymen. Here cold fact, detached method, and a scientific universe of discourse about symbolic behavior are substituted for the more usual arguments and polemics.

It may seem strange to some to refer to the treatment of Tennessee Ernie, Dinah Shore, Walter Cronkite, and their shows as "symbols" and "symbol systems." Yet such reference is as valid and correct as the commonly accepted references in these terms to Oedipus Rex and Hamlet. Both arouse and evoke feelings, beliefs, and values. The little dramas in which these television performers play do direct the mental attention of their audiences, and their outcomes do "purge" the emotions of those who watch. Their TV images "stand for and express" more than what they are, and as such are meaningful symbols that have significance and operate in important ways in American life. Their different kinds of meanings and functions to the several social groups that compose the many audiences, together with the changing role of television itself, are treated with admirable clarity, understanding, and detachment in *Living with Television*.

The social structures of simple, "primitive" societies that are little more than an organization of families, with age and sex levels that order the behavior of the members of the tribe, are matched by the simplicities of their symbol systems. Their low division of social labor is interrelated with a lack of differentiation and diversity in their symbol systems. The symbol-sharing groups usually include everyone. The common bodies of understanding are available to all and usually used by all. Moral and spiritual values, beliefs, and technological concepts are also commonly shared; a core of basic understandings is likely to spread through all activities of all members. In such simple societies, problems of maintaining unity and integration, which are implicitly part of the social burden of all symbol systems, are easily performed. Moreover, in such societies social change is minimal and the meanings of signs and symbols remain traditional and sharply defined.

The social structures, symbol systems, and character of social change in our society are the exact opposite of those found in the simple societies. In America, there is a high division of social labor with great economic and social specialization. This results in extremes of social complexity and diversity of activity. Moreover, in terms of individuals there is the greatest variety of personalities, each with its own idiosyncratic interpretations of itself and the realities around it. Instead of a few kinds of social groups, there are literally thousands. Beliefs and values are highly diverse, many in conflict and in opposition. The symbol systems, running from abstruse mathematics, the complexities of the several sciences, and the esoteric qualities of the arts through the diversities of ethnic, religious, and class affiliations on to the more commonly shared systems of the market place and everyday life, are of almost infinite variety. They exist in and serve a society undergoing rapid change, one which constantly faces disintegration and conflict and suffers from the mal-functioning of faulty communication and misinterpretation of the many meanings that appear for social recognition. As we change socially, our separate symbol systems become more diverse and less understood by more people.

No society can exist without a common core of basic understandings that are shared by all and continuously re-expressed and reinterpreted in such a way that they viably persist through time in the minds of most people. The newly invented techniques of the mass media, television among them, provide the technological channels that help maintain and change traditional understandings for all and that through time allow new knowledge, new beliefs, and new values to be disseminated among the millions and through their diversities of understanding. They can contribute, and usually do, to the maintenance of shared knowledge and shared sentiments and shared experiences necessary for social cohesion. The print of newspapers and magazines, the sound of radio, and the image of television, along with the more private sounds of telephone and telegraph are signs of meaning that are conveyed to vast audiences.

To be successful not only as profit-making organizations but also as conveyors of common meanings to most people in America, the mass media must break through the private meanings of small groups, through the many special significances of social-class levels and professional and educational groups, into ethnic derivations and interest groups, and to them bring meanings that are understandably acceptable. Many critics of television and other mass media forget that just to send symbols (such as programs) is insufficient; it is also necessary for the meanings of such media to be received, in order to complete their conveyance. Moreover, if the mass media— the Sunday newspapers, the picture magazines, or the network programs—are to perform their integrative functions, their meanings must be acceptable to large groups of people. The technologies of the mass media are recognizably capable of servicing large numbers of individuals; the symbols must have the same potential, for symbol and technique to perform their proper functions. Mass symbol systems, such as TV programs, must send basic, traditional understandings and contribute new meanings to them, or they fail to serve their primary social purpose. New knowledge, fresh beliefs and values must be properly introduced and share their place on the stage with the traditional ones for their mass audiences' edification and appreciation.

Such commonly shared symbols often are disappointing to special groups. Intellectuals complain, religious groups despair, liberals castigate, and conservatives are alarmed, yet each group usually has its own way of relating its members to the meanings of the mass media. With protest and loud complaint, each has been helped by the media of the masses to function properly as members of the great society. In the language of the authors of this book, they may be "protesters" or "accommodators," yet they do look at the images, they do listen and read, and thus—willingly or not—become members of a common group and share its common understandings. And by so doing, they are interrelated with the common flow of meanings and activities that make up the activities of a changing society.

The social characteristics of the groups of individuals and the positive and negative meanings that they attribute to the programs compose the audiences of television. In the chapters that follow, the able analyses of such audiences competently and gracefully communicate deep insight and understanding to the reader not only about television but about the America in which we live.

W. LLOYD WARNER

PART ONE

Introduction

CHAPTER ONE

A PERSPECTIVE

_____

This book is about television viewers—about how they use the medium and how they feel about it. It is organized around the idea that the television experience is best understood by analyzing and interpreting viewers' attitudes toward television's availability and content, and it emphasizes the social and psychological factors associated with viewers' relationships to the medium. The viewer remains the focus of attention throughout the book; and it is the au·thors' purpose to assess what meanings television has for him, to describe why he comes to use it as he does, and the particular ways in which he establishes a relationship with it.

While the form of presentation used is that of the essay, in which no great stress is placed on the scientific genesis of the discussion and conclusions, the ideas and concepts discussed here derive from a series of specific research studies carried out by Social Research, Inc., from 1957 to 1961. These were done for Campbell-Ewald Company, an advertising agency associated with the sponsorship of several television shows and interested in keeping in close touch with viewers' reactions to these and other programs and, more generally, with people's attitudes toward the total television scene. During a four-and-one-half-year period, sixty-nine separate studies were conducted and reported to

Campbell-Ewald Company, involving over 13,000 interviews, most often with television viewers, occasionally with nonviewers. Our sampling procedures and research methods, together with examples of our interview schedules and questions, are discussed in some detail in the appendix to this book.

Our studies were designed with specific research questions and immediate objectives in mind: What did viewers think of a particular show, of the main personalities on it, of the guest star? What did they learn from the commercials about the product advertised, and what feelings were either developed or sustained about the product? How did viewers happen to select this show for watching? What expectations did they have of the show, and in what ways and to what degree were these fulfilled? Who were the program's viewers and how did they respond to the plot? Did it hold their interest? What kind of audience involvement did it achieve, and on what basis? Are these viewers likely to watch the show again? Invariably, however, there was an opportunity to learn from each of these specific queries something of a more general order about television as a whole. It was, in fact, impossible to avoid broader considerations, for to understand the specific problems under investigation required a wider context in which to explore and to answer the individual questions being asked.

This volume deals with these more general considerations about television, referring to the findings of the individual studies only occasionally and in order to elucidate a a more general idea. It also derives from the results of an intensive survey of attitudes that obtained an overview of viewers' feelings about and uses of television. Our emphasis was placed on TV's meanings as a medium for entertainment, advertising and other kinds of communication, and the study was designed so that it was possible to assess current and emerging attitudes toward its programs and commercial content among different viewer groups. This study was carried out during the first eight months of 1960, and the results are used throughout the book.

The following chapter presents an over-all evaluation of attitudes toward television during recent seasons, in order to indicate what viewers have been thinking about it and what it has offered to its audiences during this period, in contrast to earlier experiences with the medium. A section on television's audiences follows, and each of the three chapters into which it is divided describes a particular set of feelings about television and the characteristic ways in which different audience groups use it. Television's programs and performers are the subject of the next section, and the two chapters into which it is divided refer to ten different program types and to different phases in performers' careers. A final section has to do with commercials, and these two chapters discuss what viewers think to be important elements in this type of advertising and the feelings they have about them. In an appendix to the volume we present a methodological statement, describing in more detail the research studies from which this book derives; technical procedures, sampling considerations, and questions used in the studies are presented and discussed.

The nine chapters that make up this volume touch on a variety of matters relating to television. This material differs from most works on the subject, which tend to be polemical, laden with the personal values of their authors. The present essay is relatively dispassionate; it seeks to describe the television audiences as they exist rather than to exhort them to one or another position. The authors' individual preferences (and they are not always in agreement) among programs or personalities, their views on commercials, etc., are put aside for the most part in favor of examining the spectrum of television attitudes that appear in the many interviews that form the basis of this study.

No doubt it is impossible to stand entirely aside from controversies and evaluative positions regarding television. However, the many studies used here were not oriented to testing the larger social effects of television as these may modify our society or to testing the customary hypotheses about the effects of television on children or on family life. Were child watchers more aggressive, did they read less, was adult taste corrupted? Our studies do not reveal (other than by suggestion) whether these things occurred. Rather, they show the range of people's attitudes on such social questions and suggest that these attitudes are characteristically related to other attitudes about learning, social interaction, and family well-being. It is a curious paradox that often people who assert loudly that in child-rearing it is the parents' relationships with their children that really count are also people who most fear the deleterious effects of television. Parents who truly believe that their children's character is formed out of the parent-child relationship rarely think that this resolves itself into a race for the television dial.

Because the studies for this book were authorized by advertising agencies, television sponsors, and participants in the medium, the contemporary nature of television was taken not as an opponent but as an object to be studied. The usual purpose of our research was to analyze the meanings of specific program content, the implications of particular formats, personalities, events, and stories for their audiences. The goal was not to judge whether it is better for television or society to watch Walter Cronkite on *Eyewitness to History* or Anne Baxter on *Checkmate* but to learn what is communicated by these presentations, who is disposed to watch, for what reasons, and with what reactions. We also wanted to know how commercials fit in, from the viewpoint of their integration with the program and meaningfulness to the audiences, and to judge how the sales message is received and how it affects the audiences' views of the sponsor and his products.

In putting together for this volume the immediate findings of the various specific studies plus the general study of 1960, it seemed useful to offer a distillation of many kinds of results rather than to search too diligently for a single unifying theme. To the extent that these chapters have such a theme, it is that diversity reigns. We have tried to show that there are many audiences, not merely a mass audience or a great audience or *the* television audience. There are those who embrace, protest, or accommodate to television. Sharing these broad attitudes are the many subgroups of men and women, children, teen-agers, and adults, people of different social classes, life styles, and personal aims. Their television attitudes grow out of their individual circumstances—their economic situation, the level and quality of their gratification in interpersonal relationships, and the kinds of problems that typically confront the women, teen-agers, young parents, aged, and others in our society.

To understand television from the audiences' viewpoints requires study of the audiences as people—as a woman with eight children, as a bachelor son who blushes for his mature parents' ears at a Jack Paar innuendo, as an intellectual Ph.D. who loves sports. Perhaps no one in or out of the television industry cares about these individuals as such, but they compose the many audiences. In the main, they are not blindly possessed by television, as they have so often been described. Even as children, their views have nuances; they distinguish good episodes from bad and feel freer in relation to television than they do toward many other social forces. They are willing to accept a great deal of mediocrity in television, being skeptical in general of the capacity of the world to provide much greatness; and they no more expect much "great" television than they do many "great American novels."

By and large, they seek and accept entertainment and variety, often suspecting that their own capacity to receive and appreciate greatness is limited and sporadic—and they distrust the false aspirations of socially mobile people who pretend to enjoy opera and modern art without understanding either. They are virtuous in their yearnings for education, but they trust that it will go on concomitantly with "regular television" or appear in theatrical rather than pedagogical terms. Beyond this, they hope that their children will not be taught bad things, become too excited or too absorbed, and that they may learn something from the electronic baby sitter.

We later indicate some of the many uses television has for its watchers, and how these vary among different groups. Most accept it as a modern miracle; if they are young enough, it is not so much a miracle as merely another piece of furniture—but it is furniture with a difference. It provides occupation, pleasure, many kinds of contemporary and cultural information; in its own way it is a cross-section (whether or not entirely valid or representative) of motifs, points of view, and distractions viable for the time.

The several audiences exist because needs and interests differ, because older people want to forget themselves and younger people to find themselves. Because they are seeking different things, they do not watch television in the same ways; perhaps they watch at different times, certainly they watch with different feelings and reactions. Each audience is engaged in testing the realities it knows, wants to learn, and finds characteristically stimulating, and it seeks fantasies it needs to explore or to find vicariously expressed.

The basic content of these realities and fantasies are

the facts and fictions of our lives. The news programs and the public events shows capture something of the stream of occurrences on the public scene. The regular audiences for these are large because people want to "keep up on what is going on." They are relatively smaller for the shows that inquire more closely into current events, but they are a large, anxious group when the gravity of events finds them united in civic responsibility and earnestness toward what the threatening times may require.

Other type of programs find their audiences through providing a particular blending of ideas, action, and feelings and by doing so in certain meaningful styles. The basic ingredients are the same—a reiteration of some aspect of human concern, such as how people do or do not get along together. What people are like and what they can do is at the most general level of this human interest, which turns entertainers into stars and provides audiences for variety and conversation shows. Beyond this, the audiences look for more organized expressions of what human relations are like. In an endless pursuit of the mystery of human events, the audiences want to know what happened; how did it start; who did what to whom; why; then what happened; what did it mean; how did it come out; and what was the point of it all? As in all fiction, but in convenient, animated, home-delivered capsules, television shows these things. It shows the mystery with the detachment of history; it shows it with skill and penetration, with casualness and blandness, with wit, grossness, or intensity, in Hawaii, in the Twilight Zone, or on Velvet's farm.

Audiences are selected out of the mass—and the audiences select the programs—by the particular theme and the way in which it is customarily handled. We later discuss various types of programs to indicate how content and style blend in different ways to produce audiences weighted in one direction or another. If audience diversity is one of the central themes in this book, another is that this diversity of audiences is related to the diversity of program types in consistent ways. Diversity does not mean that there is no coherence among viewers; it is possible to study television shows and see which audiences are attracted and why they have their particular composition.

People can usually predict which audiences will respond to a particular show on the basis of a projection of their own reactions. The casual assumption that Westerns are attractive to men and soap operas to women is generally true, although a considerable number of women watch Westerns with enjoyment. But audiences are not always found where such casual predictions might suggest. For example, in one study we found that the audience for *Twilight Zone* did not predict itself very well; each subgroup thought the show suitable for itself and not for others, but this was true for young people as well as adults and for people of both middle-class and lower-class social status. Because it presents an unusual combination of emotional and intellectual appeal, profound in some of the questions it asks about life and death and exciting in the way it asks them, the program is able to reach mature and thoughtful people as well as youthful seekers of stimulation. Because it is provocative and cannot answer many of the questions it raises, it loses that "average" audience who prefer to confront life's mysteries at a more practical and comprehensible level.

The choices made by various audiences are meaningful because programs are systems of symbols that express one or another set of values. In a sense, by dialing a channel a viewer dials in a symbol system. When it is one that fits his values, he feels a sense of willingness and affirmation, of interest and agreement to follow where it leads. Programs are compounds of symbolic answers to human strivings and personal problems. Those who take such problems very seriously cannot tolerate "wasting time" with comedians who make light of important matters; those who want to ride more casually over the surface of life are bored by *Mary Stuart* and *Meet the Press,* preferring entertainment that proves living to be no more troublesome than Dobie Gillis finds it. None of these attitudes are exclusive to one audience group or another, and there are extremists who watch no television at all or who watch only very specific kinds of programs. Most people range more widely, making allowance for the momentary circumstance, the other people in the room, and the temporary modifications in taste that mood may impose on their basic preferences.

Television is in a period of transition, since many contemporary forces are gathering impetus to change it. It has lost its initial and intense vitality; new attempts will be made to arouse excitement for pay TV, color, and as yet unimagined solutions to protests and criticisms. In whichever directions the medium goes, its growth and reception will be greatly modified by the extent to which it takes account of the varied needs of its different audiences.

In general, television reinforces the existing symbol systems of American society in a conserving fashion. This is not surprising, since more sponsors, writers, and broadcasting personnel are likely either to express these basic values directly or to recognize and address themselves to them. This suggests that change will be gradual, since most television audiences are unlikely to be willing or able to assimilate an upheaval in program content. At the same time, there is sufficient uneasiness and discontent, a searching for new directions, goals, and understandings of the modern world, so that bolder efforts to break away from the most traditional viewpoints will probably be rewarded. In distilling what we have learned from the many studies mentioned here, we hope that the results will transcend the time-bound aspects of these studies and contribute usefully toward shaping the as yet unknown form of television in the future.

CHAPTER TWO

TELEVISION IN TRANSITION

Television is a subject about which people have many opinions. It is familiar, popular, and public and easily becomes a topic of controversy. The variety of opinions, as well as the intensity of feeling that often accompanies these attitudes, also derives from a strong tendency to think of television in evaluative, "good or bad" terms. These may refer to its programs and personalities, whether they are liked or disliked, or they may be more general and have to do with whether television is providing the right kind of entertainment or service and whether its effects are beneficial or harmful. Usually they include what the viewer believes is happening to television, and then deal with his feelings about the changes he detects and his criticisms of things to which he is opposed.

This chapter surveys some of the more important of these opinions, attitudes, and evaluations as they were expressed by viewers during recent television seasons, beginning with 1958-59 and continuing through 1960-61. Our approach here is fairly broad and general, without at this point giving attention to television's specific content or to the divergent attitudes held by different audience groups. An examination and interpretation of these differences, which are both numerous and important, is reserved for the following three chapters, which pertain to particular segments of television's large and varied audience. Here our emphasis is placed on opinions about television as a whole, on judgments that tend to be characteristic among all groups of viewers. Any particular group may vary from this central pattern, and the pattern itself, because it represents a general tendency, does not portray exactly any single audience group. But it does serve more clearly and sharply to contrast current television with its own past and its emerging future.

A recurrent theme in all our studies is that television now is different from what it once was and, more specifically, that it no longer is as interesting, as satisfying, or as "good" as was formerly the case. This evaluation is quite consistent and is frequently expressed with considerable vigor. It almost always ignores the many individual programs and performers that a viewer enjoys, as well as the many important appeals of television and the significant meanings of the medium that are still found to be satisfying. The assertion, instead, emphasizes feelings of dissatisfaction with television as a whole, calling forth any number of individual irritations and complaints about some aspect of the medium that the viewer no longer finds satisfying to his present interests or tastes. It often finds expression in sharply critical terms, as in these direct quotations from persons interviewed:

> It sure is going down. I think that Westerns and murder have just about taken over. There's not near as many good spectacular programs as there used to be, and you have to look for a good play, something that isn't a sob-story like on daytime programs. And there's so much controversy about it going on all the time. I doubt that it will ever go out of our lives, but it won't play as important a part as it did when it was new and absorbing. Everybody you know watches it less than they did five years ago.
>
> I think the technicalities have been worked on and improved. Problems have been overcome and camera work improved. Ideas for stories and for programming have been improved.

. . . But there's more sex; I don't know if you can call it immoral exactly, but I think it is a morally degrading idea. And
I feel it will grow with television. There is more Hollywood
getting in all the time, and with Hollywood that is the natural thing.

I think they're running out of good entertainment. You see
one show and they have a person on, and a few nights later
you see that same person on another show. That's what I mean
when I say they are running out of good entertainment.
They're running out of talent to have on.

Our analysis of many such evaluations reveals a clustering around certain related ideas: programs and performances are of lower quality, current television standards are not as high, there are more (too many) commercials, and television today is generally less imaginative
and less innovative than in preceding years. Other related judgments see current TV as repetitive, with many
programs of the same genre being offered, and as more
controversial and hence less comfortable than in the past.

These complaints are not new to television; they appeared shortly after it became widely owned and
watched and have persisted in one form or another
throughout its brief history. There is reason to believe
that for years to come many of these criticisms will remain as issues of contention regardless of programming
changes. What is different now is the prevalence of these
ideas among a large majority of viewers and the consistency and intensity of their expression. Even more significant has been an increased tendency to use these evaluations as a way of explaining and justifying other feelings
about and current uses of television.

The complaint about quality is simply that TV shows
do not seem to be as good as they were. The time when
they were better is usually not precisely stated, possibly
because the viewer does not have specific programs in
mind with which he is comparing present shows. Rather,
the complaint is an evaluation of what viewers think to

be television's current offerings compared to a generalized and glorified past. When pressed to be more specific,
viewers may identity programs that were formerly des-
ignated as outstanding and popular, as representing television at its best, that served to symbolize TV for the
new and exciting entertainment it provided. Milton
Berle, Caesar and Coca, *Playhouse 90,* Ed Sullivan, *I
Love Lucy, Kukla, Fran and Ollie,* Arthur Godfrey, Dinah Shore and *The Chevy Show* are recalled and ex-
tolled in this way. Current TV offerings do not seem to
be of the same quality, even including the familiar shows
and stars that are still on the air. *Wagon Train* at one
time came close, *The Untouchables* has some of the older meanings, Jack Paar may be almost on this level,
Huntley and Brinkley in their particular sphere seem to
be much like the past greats—but the consensus is that
television no longer presents the same kinds of programs
and people. They have faded from the scene and, in so
doing, have changed television, making it less interesting and satisfying than it was. And there is an inclination to suspect that the exciting "good old days" may
never come back again.

We find dissatisfaction, too, in that television does not
seem as lively and as varied as it was. There are complaints about too many similar programs, about the same
performers appearing all the time. Too many "has-beens"
are kept on when they no longer deserve it, and the same
program idea is copied from one show to another. Variety shows don't have much variety, or the variety isn't
very new; comedy shows aren't very funny; Westerns
are pretty much the same old thing; family situation
shows are all just about alike. Television's current repetitiveness is easily translated into the idea that much of
it now is boring, at least in contrast to what it once was.
Commercials, of course, share in these criticisms: many
of them are cited as almost identical to one another,

each making similar claims and asserting that its product is best, many using what appear to be similar words, people, and techniques. And commercials are too long, too numerous, too disruptive—more so now than they used to be.

Associated with this feeling about the repetitiveness of recent television is the notion that there have been few exciting and imaginative developments that compare with the past. The one area of improvement that draws a moderate amount of mention, and, when mentioned, consistent viewer approval, has to do with increased technical proficiency—an ability to bring a better picture and to use the TV camera with what seems to be more skill and expertness than was formerly the case. With shows, however, most viewers do not perceive any such improvement; they believe that few new types have appeared during recent seasons. There have been many new individual programs, so that now there is more television from which to choose, but many of these are said to be replicas of already available types.

A few viewers say that there are now more sophisticated programs, that some of television's recent offerings have been far superior to anything in the past. Technical knowledge, larger budgets, and the accumulated experience of fifteen years of telecasting are cited in explaining this excellence. Public affairs programs and news broadcasting are frequently mentioned as examples; so, too, are discussion programs, such as *Open End* and *At Random*, and serious plays like the *Play of the Week* series and special productions such as *Macbeth*. Less often, a viewer may refer to what he considers a particularly good Western, an interesting comedy, a spectacular, as an indication of recent television at its best —but, admittedly, in its smallest amounts.

The main programming innovations that viewers comment on are adventure and detective shows, such as *The*

Untouchables, Hawaiian Eye, 77 Sunset Strip, or *The Roaring '20s.* These programs are strongly identified as television's recent offerings, and they have many fans among present viewers. But these and similar shows present aspects that incline viewers to deny their value, if not their innovative features. They are regarded as stressing the controversial issues of sex and violence, often in uncomfortable ways, so that few viewers want to think of these programs, regardlesss of how they may enjoy them, as television at its best. In this sense, such programs do not take the place of the old favorites, though they may be watched with as much or with even more faithfulness and involvement. Neither do they encourage a strong and direct identification with the performers, as did some of the earlier favorites. In the past several seasons, the trend has been for many of television's main performers to play a titled role, and the shows in which they appear are formal and stylized. For viewers, these programs may provide excellent entertainment, but they do not capture the sense of liveliness and intimacy, the "here-and-now" feeling, that many former programs had.

These and similar evaluations lead many viewers to insist that they watch television less now than before. They extend this claim to other members of their family and to their neighbors and friends. However, this idea may be at variance with more objective statistics of the amount of time that people spend watching television. The Nielsen Television Index, for example, estimates that the average number of hours of viewing per television home per day increased steadily between 1950 and 1957 from 4.5 to 5.2. It then dropped to a slightly lower level, 5.1 hours in 1958, 5.0 hours in 1959, and 5.1 hours in 1960. While this is not a measure of individual viewing time, it does suggest that the beliefs of the viewers about how much time they spend watching television now as compared with previous years may be under-estimated. But the attitude is crucial, for it reveals an attempt to detract from the importance of this activity and to claim that it means less than it once did.

In this connection, recent television seasons have brought to the fore a growing embarrassment about watching television—at least, about watching what is thought to be "too much TV." In the current set of pro-prieties that surround television watching, it is no longer considered fashionable to state that you watch it a lot, or that you watch it very regularly or very intensely. Neither should you have many favorite programs, nor is it quite proper to display a high level of acceptance of TV or much excitement about it. When people contrast their present TV habits with their past behavior, they reveal this embarrassment and may be inclined to exaggerate their present "distance" from television. The following quotation is a case in point:

> I sure can remember when we got our first set. I can remember racing home to watch. The first thing I saw was a soap opera on it. No, no, it was a give-away program, Happy Jack Somebody. He had a mustache, one of those audience participation programs. It was for women, Jack Somebody-or-other. I remember he had a mustache. It was *Queen for A Day!* That was it, Happy Jack, a man with a mustache. And it was like that for several weeks: rush home to see it. The next stage was you watched everything while you were home but didn't race home. From then on I watched when I had the time only. It was a week, maybe longer, when I'd race home. The next period lasted a couple of months and I'd sit in front of the thing every night, shove the kids out of the way so I could watch it. I'd like shows the first few times and then I couldn't stand it. Wrestling was good, too. And Jack Webb's *Dragnet.* I liked it at first. We bought it because it was like buying a new car, maybe more so. It was new and different. I bought it for myself, for the sports. I wish I felt now about television like I did when I bought my first one. I spent $420 on that set! I'll never forget it, it still eats on me whenever I think of it! Four hundred and twenty dollars! Now I wouldn't spend $150. But then to think of the World Series being on and me not able to watch it!

Descriptions of television prior to the past three seasons, and especially of television at the time sets were first purchased, capture a deep sense of awe, wonderment, and pleasure, often mixed with a considerable amount of gratitude. Television, for most viewers, meant wonderful entertainment, a new and exciting world of people and ideas, a new range of experiences and emotions, all as easily within grasp as the knob on one's set. It was novel and different, and the viewer went about getting his fill of it, spending what he now recalls as a great deal of time watching programs, learning what television had to offer, slowly selecting his favorites, and gradually developing his personal preferences and quality standards.

During the past several television seasons it has become apparent that TV is now a much more taken-for-granted activity. It no longer has the same degree of glamor or attraction of five and ten years ago. It is no longer new or novel, and people do not find it nearly so exciting or awesome, and sometimes not as pleasurable, either. They now are inclined to approach it in what they believe to be more sensible and selective ways.

Our studies show also that viewers are inclined to think of TV in new relationships to other values, activities, and styles of living. One developing trend that reflects this modification in attitude is a shifting of the TV set from the living room to the family room, the recreation room, or the bedroom. This is more pronounced among those of higher-status, upper-middle-class owners but is by no means restricted to these people; sets are being moved from the home's public and prominently displayed locations to its more private, casual, utilitarian, and convenient parts. As one man commented, expressing his present views on television together with some of his attitudes on familial relations, "We now have the TV in the basement for the kids. I feel that to have it in the living room would be like having a loud-mouthed mother-in-law in there all the time. It would be just a nuisance." In a similar way, viewers claim that other leisure activities have become more inviting and therefore more competitive with television. These include other forms of entertainment—"Instead of watching so much television we now go out more than we used to" is a fairly common way of putting it—as well as hobbies and sports that provide enjoyment and relaxation and at the same time require more energetic activity and evoke less personal uneasiness than "watching so much TV."

Underlying many of the criticisms people make of television, their diminished interest in it, and their claim that they watch it less and use it differently, are several additional factors. One is that there is now a greater understanding of television—what it offers, how it works, what standards it follows, how it is best used—and during recent television seasons this has come to be a more important determinant of viewers' feelings. A backlog of experience forms the basis of this knowledge; there is a TV past with which people are familiar and which they take into account when viewing and judging current offerings. There are the television guides and weeklies, the daily columnists, and the program advertising that viewers are exposed to and make use of, all of which add to their information. Older programs and personalities have come to be known more intimately, and newer shows and stars are learned about more quickly, if only because viewers know what to look for and have past guides and standards to go by. As a consequence, television tastes in recent years have become better formulated and viewers are more discriminating in what they watch and in what they want.

Viewers have come to expect more of television, and their standards for evaluating its content are substantially higher than they used to be. Programs that seemed novel, interesting, or unusual when first presented have come to be judged as not good enough. These attitudes have made it more difficult for television to entertain people, and in place of the earlier attentive and respectful viewing patterns there is now a prevalent feeling among those viewers we interviewed that "TV has the obligation to keep me entertained."

"Entertainment" in connection with television emerges as a broadly defined concept. It is, of course, the first and foremost of television's meanings and sources of strength. It pertains to shows of many types and stars of many kinds, excitement, diversion, laughs, and drama. Hollywood and Broadway are expected to be represented, but so, too, are Washington, Paris, London, and Moscow. Music and dance (popular and classical), conversation and recitation, all form part of this idea. And it includes commercials, also, ranging from product presentations to animated cartoons and stories based on highly emotional themes.

Crucial to this definition of television as entertainment is the point of view of the viewer. He comes to television expecting to be entertained, which means that he will sit back and let the activity on the screen provide him with fun and relaxation. He also expects—in fact, he often assertively demands—that there be a variety of entertainment from which to choose. After he makes the initial selection of a particular program, it becomes the responsibility of the program to let him enjoy it knowingly. He is more of a "wise guy," harder to take unawares. And, in these respects, television is said to have been less satisfying during the past few years than it once was.

The viewer has thus become more demanding, and part of this is related to his greater self-awareness as a member of an audience that is important. Increasingly, during recent years, people who watch television and who know something about the system by which it works have begun to see themselves as part of a discriminating audience that selects particular shows and forgets about others, that causes some stars to stay on and others to go off the air, that determines which products are bought and which are not. Rating systems, while fairly remote in their exact operation for most viewers, are known and discussed and probably of some circular influence in this connection. More important, the viewers' sense of expertness has become quite widespread. Evaluations of programs and commercials are made, not only in terms of "I like this" or "I don't like that," but also by more precise quality standards. And, looking into the future, the viewer is likely to gain in self-awareness as expert and judge, at least to the extent that he becomes still more selective and discriminating in his television tastes.

It is these attitudes of television's audience that provide some of the basic dynamics for change in TV's content, format, and style. There recurs in our interviews the constant theme of wanting more and different programs and, on the other side of the coin, of gradually tiring of the old ones. Constantly there is a process of revision of judgment of shows and personalities, in part because of the competition among the stars and programs already on the air and in part because the viewer is getting used to and tiring of the old and the familiar.

TV, judged by how the audience feels about it and approaches it, is an avid consumer of talents and shows and commercials. It is also an avid consumer of techniques and styles and formats. This is a continuous and repetitive processs, with newness and novelty attracting attention and familiarity resulting in boredom and lack of interest. Of course, television has encouraged these attitudes by responding to them. It has provided newness, and, regardless of how satisfying this is ultimately found to be, the new does compete with the old for viewers' loyalties. In this way, television itself upholds the notion that it must always stimulate and satisfy and that the new is likely to do this more than the old.

An assessment of these recently developed attitudes suggests that, from the viewer's perspective, television has been and continues to be in a transition phase. The transition has been from a ten-year period of rapid growth, from a high level of excitement about TV and widespread acceptance of all that it offered, to a period marked by uneasiness, dissatisfaction, denial, and criticism. The present phase is one in which viewers are attempting to redefine what television means to them and in which they are struggling to learn how to use it in new and different and more satisfying ways.

Even as this process continues—as it will for several years to come—television remains an important and appealing medium for the vast majority of set owners. Though people feel differently about it now, it nevertheless continues to function as a vital and vigorous vehicle for entertainment, communication, stimulation, relaxation, and a variety of other personal and social gratifications. Easy to meet, flexible in how and when and why it can be used, it is still watched by almost everyone who owns a set. With a diversity of content and attractions, and meaningful to different people in different ways, it continues to affect most Americans very directly and repetitively.

Television is a medium whose influence pervades all areas of life. At present it functions in many ways at once for most Americans, entertaining and teaching, informing and pleasing, occupying time, demanding attention, providing ideas and models of thought, behavior, and attitude. In its social meanings, television serves as a moral force, acts as an authority, and at one and the same time works to unify our society and to pull apart different segments of it. On a personal level, it sets standards, develops expectations, and encourages fantasies. It produces and then allows for the discharge of many kinds of feelings and emotions. It does all these things for all types of men and women, of different ages and status, for each in pertinent ways because of the diversity of its content and the flexibility of its mode of presentation.

But television's problems during this transition phase are also apparent, and these are not likely to diminish in the next few years. In fact, they will probably increase, as viewers become still more selective in their choices and habits. This trend is already discernible and promises to be augmented as television becomes yet more familiar and subject to even more criticism during the next few seasons.

Selectivity means less watching for watching's sake and more a seeking-out of known programs for their special qualities and appeal. It means using guides and references in helping to select programs, and it implies that programs will increasingly have to fit into people's life styles and activity patterns as well as into their particular moods and tastes. Selectivity points to an increased knowledge of different program types and of specific shows and especially to the development of loyalties toward certain programs so that they are tuned in week after week. Program loyalty thus is likely to increase in coming years, though the numbers of shows any single viewer may watch will be smaller than at present and in the past, and it implies a strong identification with and seeking-out of particular stars and personalities. Similarly, selectivity suggests new expectations of television advertising and new interpretations of its influences on audiences. With viewers watching the same shows more frequently and consistently, repetitive exposure to the products advertised is likely to take on considerable significance in evaluating a show's advertising worth.

For these reasons, gross measurement of the size of the total audience will be a less valuable guide for evaluating programs in the future. It will become more important to know who the viewers are and what their relationship to a show is, their special reasons for favoring it, and the more nearly unique kinds of gratifications they seek from it. It will become more meaningful to conceive of a "core audience" for each show—a group of people who respond most fully and reliably to each distinctive program—and to examine in terms of this core what a program does for the products it advertises. It is also likely that smaller but more appropriate audience groupings will become a conscious goal of producers and advertisers alike, as selection comes to dominate the relation between viewer and program. This prognosis implies that in coming years there may be less television watching but that the quality of viewing may become more intense. And, finally, these and related trends signify that further changes in the meanings, uses, and appeal of television are likely to come to the fore and that these will continue to evoke new responses to the medium.

These changes will generally reflect the basic directions of change in our society itself. Television is an outstanding arena for contending social values. Because it is a deeply attractive and unusually pervasive medium and because its utilization is supposed to be in the public interest, it cannot be left alone. The populace is free to ignore the newspapers, magazines, motion pictures, and Broadway shows of which it disapproves; influential minorities can support any one of these activities adequately while the rest more or less go their way. But the public, insistent character of television, its privileged position in the home, and the relatively narrow range of choice available on it at any given time give everyone the "right" to have outspoken views about it. As a consequence, critical groups are less willing to let it go its own way than they are the other media. Television seems too great a potential social force to ignore—or to let others tamper with—when it is not satisfying. Consequently, some people want not merely to censor but to impose their ideas of superior programing much more vigorously than they do on the other media. This is clearly a matter about which different audience groups take different positions, as the following chapters indicate.

PART TWO

Television's Audiences

It has been commonplace to think of television's viewers in essentially unitary terms, as a single audience, a homogeneous group of viewers, a large group of people who are simultaneously exposed to the same program and commercial stimuli. Even descriptions of audience composition tend to focus on characteristics of the entire group, such as age, sex, occupation, income, or education, with little attention being given to major audience segments, to distinct modes of watching television, to particular and persistent sets of attitudes toward its content.

The limitations inherent in this unitary concept of viewers becomes more apparent as set ownership becomes commonplace and as the number of viewers increases to include almost all Americans. The idea of a single audience could be tolerated when there were fewer channels and only 660,000 TV homes, as was the case in 1949, and even when there were 30 million such households, as in 1955. But by 1961, 88 per cent of all American homes had a television set, and the 49,900,000 TV homes and approximately 160 million people represented by this figure make it much more difficult to think of all viewers as comprising a single audience.

The limitations of this concept also become clearer as attitudes toward television change. This has occurred in the past several TV seasons as television has become less novel and as program tastes and preference have become more sharply defined. Under these conditions, the advantage in learning more about the important divisions within this large audience is self-evident. The same is true when viewers are more critical of television, when they seem to be harder to attract to particular shows, when program mortality is on the rise, when advertisers get to be more reluctant to asssume program sponsorship —conditions that have increasingly come to the fore in the past several years and that have given impetus to getting new kinds of information about television viewers.

The research on which this book is based was organized largely in terms of individual viewers and the subjective experience of owning a television set, of watching television, of having to make program selections, of being exposed to advertising. The fact that a person happened to be a viewer (or a nonviewer, as the case may be) was taken as a starting point rather than as a research finding. In this way, the overt behavior of watching TV became, as such, much less significant to the analysis, and our attention was directed toward the attitudes and feelings surrounding the act of watching.

Subjective experience, as differentiated from behavior itself, is by no means the only criterion for classifying and analyzing television viewing and television viewers, but it is a useful one in that it touches upon a wide range of theoretical and practical problems. It offers the possibility of bringing to bear valuable sociological and psychological interpretations; it has the advantage of placing television in a cultural setting and stressing the social meanings and functions of this medium and its symbolic content. Further, it places the viewer in a key role, as the individual who selects, watches, responds to, and evaluates what he sees, always in an interpersonal context of viewer and medium.

Examined from this point of view, it is evident that watching television is a different sort of experience for different people. It becomes clear that there is no single audience group and that a unitary mode of defining television's audience is overly restrictive. There are at least several audiences, each with a particular point of view toward the medium. These points of view each include a distinctive set of feelings about television, characteristic ways of using it, and a unique manner of selecting, responding to, and evaluating its content.

In this part of the book three such viewpoints are discussed. The first is referred to as "television embraced"; it signifies a particularly close identification with television, a rather undiscriminating and accepting attitude toward it, and, usually, great use of the medium. In contrast, "television protested" is an audience outlook that signifies the most selective use of the medium and often extremely critical attitudes toward it. "Television accommodated" is a position that rather casually accepts television, one that evidences a "coming to terms" with TV, its meanings, appeals, and shortcomings. As suggested by the descriptive phrase, television is well integrated into the life styles and the psychosocial needs and values of viewers who adopt this stance.

These three sets of attitudes are not distributed at random among television viewers. They cluster in significant patterns and are closely related to other variables that differentiate people. Most generally, each is correlated with a particular type of life style and life stage. Social status, age, familial relationship, and sex are key variables that combine to create a distinctive relationship of viewer and television. The over-all pattern is summarized by the chart on page 45.

"Television embraced" and "television protested" emerge as the polar positions, the extreme attitudes, providing the sharpest outlines for this framework of analysis. The "accommodating" attitude falls between and to some extent overlaps the other two. Each of the three is discussed in a separate chapter in this section, each discussion beginning with a general descriptive and analytical statement that highlights the main, distinctive features of the position. This is followed by a discussion of the particular audiences adopting the position, indicating why they use and feel about television in this characteristic way. Not all audiences are covered, and, of those that are, not all are given equal attention. This is due in part to the limitations of our data and in part because these different audiences are not of the same importance for understanding the viewer's relations with television. In all instances, the points made deal with the most general attitudes, ignoring the many qualifications and exceptions that a more detailed analysis would make possible and necessary.

	Upper Middle Class*	Lower Middle Class*	Upper Lower Class*
Homebound young (Children to 12)	Embraced	Embraced	Embraced
Teen-agers (13-20 years)	Protested	Protested	Protested
Family years: Child-rearing (20-35)	Protested	Accommodated	Embraced
Homemaking (35-55 years)	Protested	Accommodated	Embraced
Homebound old (over 55)	Embraced	Embraced	Embraced

*As used in this book, the term "class" has a very specific meaning; it defines a group of people who conform to a number of criteria based on many investigations of social class structure. A "social class" is composed of those people who occupy a particular position which is the product of such elements as income, education, formal and informal relationships (as in clubs and churches), type of housing and neighborhood, etc. The three major social class groupings in our samples may be described briefly. The *upper middle class* are the predominantly managerial and professional groups, generally regarded as educated and sophisticated. They live in suburbs and better residential areas. They take college education for granted and are strongly oriented toward career achievements. They constitute approximately 12% of the population. The *lower middle class* are the small business owners, minor executives, white collar workers, and some skilled blue collar people. They are stable and home-oriented, devoted to practical and moral goals. About 35% of the population are in this classification. The *upper lower class* are those engaged in service occupations and blue collar activities. Many live in industrial, urban areas and live within rather sharply limited horizons of work and family. They constitute approximately 40% of the population.

CHAPTER THREE

TELEVISION EMBRACED

"*Television* embraced" is the point of view that has been traditionally and most frequently associated with this medium. It is composed of attitudes toward and characteristic uses of television indicating an intimate bond between the viewer and his set. It implies a strong and general acceptance of television, with abundant use, great familiarity, considerable enjoyment, and a profound sense of gratitude for its presence and availability. The embracing attitude has been in the past and still remains the most prevalent of viewer stances, though, like all aspects of television, it has undergone change and continues to be modified as the meaning and content of television itself changes.

The Characteristics of Embrace

The embracing attitude must first be distinguished from a highly stereotyped, exaggerated, and yet widely accepted view of how a majority of people use and feel about television. What might be described as an "overly embraced" version pictures millions of Americans sitting docilely before their sets, hour after hour, night after night, day after day. Time has little relevance; outside interests and activities are minimal; television is dominant for the person and for the family, so that there is little verbal contact even between people sitting in the same room watching the same program. Television supposedly alters most personal relations, diminishes one's energies, sharply modifies values, and works to dull the senses. The overly embracing attitude consists of indiscriminate and avid viewing and a passive if deeply involved participation in program content. Television so portrayed is all entertainment. Intellectual stimulation is practically nonexistent, and the emotions and fantasy produced within the viewer tend to be primitive and base. According to this notion, standards of quality are extremely low and the viewer's primary goal is to get more and more satisfaction with less and less effort.

There is no evidence that this stereotype was ever a valid representation or interpretation of what went on between viewer and television, though the point of view seems always to have had a large number of adherents, especially among television's critics. Of course, there are many truthful elements in this portrayal, but the conception is grossly overdrawn; it is a caricature and cannot be seriously considered.

It is instructive to speculate why this conception of television and its audience has been so acceptable. Among the many possible explanations, the moral implications of the attitude appear to be important; it involves an implicit judgment of both the medium and the viewer. It depicts television as consisting entirely of stimulation of an undesirable sort and shows most viewers succumbing to the hypnotic and emotional appeal of the medium. It stresses the enticing quality of the medium, and it emphasizes that watching it is self-indulgent and involves a loss of self-control. The fact that television is so pleasure-dominated is also underscored by this belief, and the moral evaluation accompanying this phenomenon is decidedly negative. Thus, characterizing television in this exaggerated manner makes it easier to judge it in simple, dichotomous terms, such as "good-bad," "productive-wasteful," "socially valuable-socially destructive," with the judgment going consistently in an unfavorable direction.

The popularity and prevalence of the overly embracing definition is also accounted for by the history of television as a mass-market commodity and leisure-time activity. It is probable that in the early 1950's, when television first became available to large numbers of people, each new owner went through an intensive phase of indulging, experimenting, learning, and eventually coming to terms with the new medium. This was both an individual and a family matter. There were also ramifications on a community level, for the development of the television market caused major shifts in the uses of other institutions, and many of these shifts seemed to be associated with time spent with television to the exclusion of other interests and activities.

Still another factor explaining the ready acceptance of an exaggerated version of the embracing attitude is that overt behavior is so easily confused with subjective experience. The hours obviously spent in front of the set are assumed to signify complete subservience to television, if only because the viewer appears to be so engrossed, reluctant to leave, and apparently enjoying what he sees. It is not, however, the number of hours spent watching television that is the important indicator of the embracing point of view but, rather, a distinctive set of attitudes that characterize a particular quality of use made of television. What television means to the individual, with what feelings, values, and opinions it is typically used, and how it is integrated into one's life are the more crucial factors that differentiate the embracing attitude from others.

The most general of these distinguishing features is

that television is regarded as a part of modern living and, more particularly, as a part of one's own daily life. Watching television is similar to other normally habitual and routine activities. It is defined much like eating and sleeping, working and going to school, tending house and visiting the corner bar, shopping, and reading the daily newspapers. The essential quality of the act for those who embrace the medium is that it is a well-defined "thing," a part of one's normal daily activities, so much so that usually there is not much about watching TV that is either self-conscious or planned. The rhythm of daily life is marked by television, and a well-ordered sequence of programs contributes to a sense of ongoing time and patterned existence. When television is talked about, it immediately falls into a pattern of the things that the viewer and his family regularly do.

> There are three of us in the family, my wife and I, and Nancy who's six. She's in kindergarten. In my spare time I like to play golf and cards, work in the yard on the lawn; I like to go to sporting events, have house parties, visit with the neighbors. I spend a lot of time on my duties for the Knights of Columbus. And we watch television regularly. Nancy always watches it early in the morning and in the early evening. My wife watches soap operas at noontime and at night. We watch more in winter than in summer. We watch every day, between us about five or six hours a day. My wife watches the *Guiding Light* and *Search for Tomorrow*. Nancy watches *Captain Bob, Captain Kangaroo, Romper Room, Big Brother, Uncle Gus, Rex Trailer, Life of Riley, Ozzie and Harriet, Leave It to Beaver*, and she also likes *Cannonball*. As for me, I regularly watch *Maverick, Cheyenne, Bourbon Street, Adventures in Paradise, Wagon Train, The Price Is Right, I've Got a Secret, This Is Your Life, The Untouchables, Zane Grey Theater, Perry Mason, Twentieth Century, Series 60, Mr. Lucky*. My wife and I like the same programs, although my wife would rather watch musicals like Perry Como. What we watch depends on who is on TV and who is busy at home and who isn't watching television. I'd say our time is split about evenly between television and other activities.

Television is not immediately discussed by its embracers in terms of individual programs and personalities (though these are important points of identification) but as a category of behavior and time spent—"We watch television everyday," "I always have TV on in the morning," or "After dinner the set goes on and we watch until 10:15." These are common ways of expressing a particular mode of relationship with the medium.

> In our leisure time we like to sing and dance. The children like to play games and cards. Two of the girls take piano lessons. They go to the YWCA and belong to the Brownies. They have to practice piano every day. The girls sing as a trio and have appeared in shows and on auditions. And besides going to school, they have church activities and they also like to watch TV. I think the girls watch TV about two hours a day and the boys watch it quite a bit more—maybe four hours a day. I may watch it three to four hours a night. My husband usually watches it before he goes to work in the afternoon. Sometimes he watches the late movie when he comes home from work.

> The boys watch TV in the morning every day. I watch it every noontime and my husband watches the 1 P.M. movie, the *Hollywood Theater*, every day. I watch the soap opera in the late afternoon every day. I have a sister who won't answer her telephone if you call while she is watching a soap opera. Since my husband has been remodeling the house, he doesn't watch as much television as he did before . . . .

The sense of television as one of many alternative activities with which it competes for the viewer's time and attention is minimal in this and similar expressions of the embraced attitude. One does not immediately perceive that programs compete with each other, for selectivity, at least at first glance, seems to be incidental to "just watching." This is not altogether correct, as will be indicated, but with the embracing outlook the importance of a specific program or star as an inducement to watch is de-emphasized. A main gratification derived from television is simply in watching, regardless of content, and it is only as a more or less secondary consideration that program choices are made.

Embracing television in this manner means that a considerable amount of time is spent watching it. There is, of course, variation on this score, but, typically, viewing is in big blocks of time—two or three hours at a stretch is not at all uncommon. And the set may be on for longer periods, with the viewer (or viewers) going away from and coming back to it at intervals.

This point of view in general minimizes most criticisms of the medium. The viewer's feeling is more likely to be one of thankfulness that TV is available and willingness to accept whatever deficiences it might have. Those who embrace television are aware of the popular criticisms, but they do not strike a meaningful chord, for the most part. It is not that these viewers are unwilling to accept negative values or that they doubt the validity of the charges. Rather, they do not see the criticisms as part of the television they watch and enjoy, and in the context of watching a specific show and in terms of the feelings they have about television, such issues seem remote and unreal.

The embracing attitude carries with it an extensive familiarity with television's offerings. These viewers are people who are conversant with what is on their sets, though less so with what is going on in and about the television world. They have their favorite shows, they know when they are on and who the stars are; they have a sense of what is popular and current, since this is the subject of discussion with their friends and relatives, but their viewing is not determined by what is most popular. Their judgments are relatively casual, placid expressions of what they like, and their inclination is to reject the standards of others, especially if these others are distant and unknown figures. Television critics, for example, are not given much heed; their world is felt to be too different from the one experienced by the viewer.

> I don't know, the TV critic in the paper and I never agree. If he likes a show, I don't like it. If he didn't like it, I liked it. He doesn't seem to know what he is talking about. The critics cannot speak for the public, they can only speak as individuals and in regard to their own taste.

This attitude may easily be assumed to reflect an indiscriminate approach to and use of television, with little deliberate choice made and little preference for one program over another. But this is to confuse the way these people watch television generally and how they watch and feel about particular programs. Their approach to the medium as a whole is, as indicated, one of watching in blocks of time. Evening viewing, for example, is a matter of turning the set on early (assuming it has not been on since late afternoon when the children were watching) and keeping it on until bedtime. But the programs that appear during this prolonged interval are dealt with in an individual manner, each one being known, evaluated, and generally responded to as a particular program that offers its own kinds of gratifications to the viewer.

If the abstract criticisms of television are minimized by those who embrace it, criticisms having to do with particular and familiar programs are not. In this more specific context, a diverse range of popular television topics can become the subjects of strong stands.

> We like most of the programs on TV but I think they could do away with all quiz programs and panel shows because they are a waste of time and are all fixed. The public is gullible but not stupid. The panel always waits to the last minute to discover the person, like on *What's My Line?* . . .

> Some programs are too repetitious, like *The Untouchables*. It's the same thing over and over, and yet we watch it. It's always exciting and that is probably the reason why . . . .

> Sometimes we are disappointed in the shows that they give too much advance publicity to. Some of the spectaculars are built up too much and then you are disappointed . . . .

One of the best shows I've seen was *Alas Babylon*. It was all about the atomic bomb and it impressed all of us. It's the kind of program that should be repeated . . . . One spectacular that I looked forward to and was quite disappointed in was Art Carney and it wasn't too good. I guess it was *Alice in Wonerland* . . . .

The TV shows that I don't like are the Westerns. I hate them and they aren't good for the children. All that shooting and killing and fighting. I know that the children imitate those cowboys and they act wild after they see a Western. They see them only against my better judgment. The Westerns are as bad as those movies about prehistoric monsters and I don't want them watching them . . . . There is one Western that I like and so do the children. That is *Wagon Train*. The people seem human, they have big stars and there seems to be some human in it.

As these comments indicate, those who embrace television are able to move through their likes and dislikes with ease, confident in their taste and secure in their own judgment. They willingly single out one show for praise, another for rebuke, and a third for what they see as an ideal for the medium to follow.

Several bases for program preference are characteristic of "television embraced." One is continuity of program; the quality of continuity, even repetition, is important to these viewers. They are people who readily become involved with a TV series. They like the opportunity to identify with a particular set of characters to the point where a sense of familiarity develops and sustains their interest and involvement. Knowing the recurring people, their relationships, and what is likely to happen—the set patterns of events and relations that so often typify television series—is of value to them. Variation on a theme is desired, but too much change in theme is likely to disrupt their ability to identify with the program or series. Such viewers often enjoy seeing reruns, watching humorously and knowingly, secure in their familiarity with the machinations of the plot and its outcome.

The attitude of these embracers is that television is supposed to relax and to engross them. It is primarily if not exclusively an entertainment medium, and this means it should not be too complicated or involved. It also should avoid being emotionally or intellectually challenging. These appeals are not unique to those who embrace television, for they are part of the medium's attractiveness to all viewers. It is rather that, with these particular viewers, such qualities have an especially important role and account for their distinctive uses of television.

The embracing attitude is accompanied by a receptive stance. The viewer is expected to be able to sit back and enjoy; the stimulation is expected to come from the set, with the viewer contributing little by way of initial interest and exitement. The viewer does not expect to work at watching. Programs are therefore judged severely, and often in "either-or" categories. Either the show succeeds in capturing and holding the viewer's attention or it doesn't; in the former case it is judged "good" and in the latter "bad."

The embracing outlook is associated with time in interesting and distinctive ways. On the one hand, it involves extended periods of watching; the television set in the home of those using it in this manner is apt to be on for hour after hour with someone usually sitting in front of it or at least listening to it. At the same time, the definition of television that is associated with this attitude is one that emphasizes the momentary qualities of the medium. Gratification is expected to be immediate, and any feeling of delay in the satisfaction it provides is a cause of quick criticism. Embracers are impatient, and they want their television to come rapidly to the point, be it in the action of stories, the dramatic quality of personalities, or the variety of entertainers. The immediate and the obvious are most appreciated.

Television's ability to distract is also particularly important to the embracer. Those who adopt this viewpoint are often people with few inner resources that would lead them to cultivate other "outside" interests and activities. For reasons of age, personality, or style of life, they are people who seek activities that can easily be picked up and engaged in without much effort on their part. Simply turning a switch and having available entertainment and a focus of attention from an object that demands little from them is admirably suited to these requirements.

The Embracers of Television

The embracing outlook is associated with three main audiences: The homebound young, the homebound old, and the working class. Each is large in size, and each is important in determining the success of most of television's major programs. Each of these audiences relates to television in essentially the same way, not because of qualities inherent in the medium but rather because their similar life styles or circumstances or their manner of seeking out and utilizing external stimuli have common elements.

The Homebound Old: The Years Alone

In contemporary America it seems increasingly unstylish, unnecessary, uneducated, and even selfish to grow old. People are not respected for their age but for the way they "handle" it, and there are a variety of inducements to handle it in better, less obvious, younger ways. And yet it can be a heavy burden trying to keep up, with a body that is less responsive, with interests that are considerably weaker, and with an attention span and an alertness that are diminished. At this stage in life there is likely to be more time but less inclination to keep occupied, as well as fewer social, emotional, and financial resources with which to accomplish this.

Television admirably fits this situation. It becomes a steady and engrossing companion. It is available at the will of the viewer, turned on or off as his feelings suggest at the moment. It fills time, it entertains, and it informs; it has a youthfulness of its own that easily and pleasantly distracts. And it can be watched very much as the viewer desires, with intensity or casualness, with involvement or haphazardly. It is no wonder, then, that older people exemplify the embracing attitudes toward and uses of television in the most clear-cut, unequivocal manner:

> Since the kids are grown I haven't had much to do. I don't do sewing or knitting, and I never did read much, not even the newspaper. Shopping isn't much fun anymore, and I don't think I ever did like to shop much. You might say (laughing) that I've been waiting for television to come along.

> Television is old people's best friend and helps pass many lonely hours. They can lose themselves in TV and not think about themselves. I agree that TV keeps us young. Just watching different advertisements keeps us up to date, also the current styles in living, clothing, and housing. It does all this and more for me.

> It keeps a person busy and his mind off himself, and keeps you from feeling sorry for yourself. Actually, I don't know what I would do without it.

> Even when you can go out, and you do have the money to do things—well, you don't always feel like getting up and getting dressed. When you get older you enjoy sitting more.

People such as these, in their late fifties and sixties, recognize that they are highly dependent on television for many things. They are aware that it has made aging in general and their own situation in particular much more "tolerable." It has served as a barrier against or an anesthetic for many of their most prominent concerns about aging. Some of television's main functions for this audience are these:

It "takes your mind off yourself" and provides an opportunity to become engrossed, diminishing self-concern and self-awareness.

It is always there, like a baby sitter, cutting through silence and loneliness and available at the turn of a button.

The day and the week can be organized around special and favorite programs, and much time can be spent watching any kind of program at all.

It feeds self-esteem and keeps people alert and informed; this is especially important for older people eager not to feel "left out" and behind the times.

It helps to socialize, providing topics for conversation as well as something to offer the children, younger people, or friends when they come to visit.

It is easy, undemanding, relaxing.

Television is almost a panacea for old age, and for this reason it is ardently embraced. While some are ashamed to admit it, most of the elderly viewers have the comfort of feeling that it is one activity they share with just about everybody else and that it is a vigorous and popular activity at that. It seems uniquely designed to dull the edges of idleness and concern, to keep the elderly alert, interested, and in contact with things, events, life itself.

If these people are "addicted," they are living in a world in which it seems a harmless addiction and one that promises to get more interesting as it goes along. It may help reduce money expended for doctors and medication; it probably helps to keep intra-family crises and recriminations from bubbling up; it saves money for people on pensions; it is an ever-ready spectacle, a slice of life, and a close companion. For most elderly people, television is a very good friend, often one of the best they have.

The older people's viewing patterns tend to be regular and entrenched; most of them know what they want to watch and watch these programs systematically. In fact, for many of these viewers a large part of their satisfaction stems from the recurring programs and people they can plan to meet. It derives from the regularity of their viewing habits, from getting familiar with the stars, the format, the situation, and the products advertised.

The women interviewed among this group are as familiar with daytime programing as with evening shows. Men who are retired and spend considerable time in the home often join their wives in watching certain daytime programs, though men tend to take a stronger stand for getting to see "their own" shows.

By and large, older people prefer shows that do not come too early in the day or too late at night. They like shows that are of half-hour duration, except for musical variety, which they feel can hold their interest for an hour. They want shows that are not especially complex or intense, that do not have to be followed with much concentration; they like to walk away a bit, snooze a bit, and return to the set without too much loss of continuity. They like a program that seems comfortably episodic, that is a story in itself even if part of a series; unfinished business is threatening for them. They like shows that have tempo and pace, that are fully peopled and offer much to view as well as hear, allowing for some slight disability in both or either of these senses.

Weekends for the elderly seem more active and peopled than weekdays, especially during the daylight hours. The weekly shopping excursion, errands to get ready for the weekend, church, visits with family and friends, auto rides in the nice weather, all break into television viewing patterns. By Sunday evening, and more or less for the rest of the week, they are ready and very willing to return to their more accustomed and less demanding television life.

Attitudes toward programs vary, of course, but by and large they run along the following lines:

News: These programs are not enjoyed most, but they are important for "keeping up."

Family situation comedies and dramas: These typically permit nostalgia and remembrance. They provide a chance to relive, relearn, and remember one's own past, trials and tribulations, loves and fears.

Comedy of the "old school": Red Skelton is a favorite, and so are Jack Benny and Bob Hope. Anyone who is and does what is reminiscent of the "good old vaudeville days" is enjoyed.

Psychological ("sick") comedy and drama: These shows are not enjoyed. Some of them are too tense and intense, making the elderly feel depressed, introspective, and lonely.

Westerns: "Boys will be boys," even at a late stage in life, and the men enjoy the Westerns. *Gunsmoke, Maverick,* and *Bonanza* especially seem to receive entrenched and entranced viewing.

Musical variety: The "pretty music" programs are enjoyed, especially when they also hark back to the old days and permit nostalgia and easy, soft relaxation. Lawrence Welk was an almost universal Saturday night favorite with this group, especially among the women.

Sports: Even for this age group, sports are the men's prerogative and many women's bane.

Movies: The elderly tend to shy away from movies because of their length. The up-to-dateness of TV is denied by these shows, though an occasional old-time movie is enjoyed and can bring back pleasant memories.

Audience participation and quiz shows: Older people often seem to have difficulty in keeping up with quick, unstructured repartee, and especially with the more subtle innuendoes on shows like Jack Paar's. They call many of them vulgar and do not find them appealing.

The Working Class:
Child-rearing and Homemaking Years

Early in its history television was defined as "one of the good things in life," and this became an inducement to acquire a set and thereby to obtain a valued object. This was especially true among working-class people, that large, respectable, and relatively stable segment of the American population that invariably becomes involved in any kind of mass behavior. As for TV, as it came to be called with an implicitly informal and endearing quality, the working class responded to it with enthusiasm. They received it as a modern miracle. More than for any other population segment, television for these people was and continues to be instrumental in bringing into their homes a new, different, and exciting world, the marvel of motion pictures domesticated.

To a large extent the rapidity with which television became a widely owned instrument is accounted for by the working-class reaction to it and the speed with which they purchased their sets. It was these people who first congregated in their corner taverns to see the early programs, and it was these people who became the early fans and the mass audience so necessary to the medium.

The history of television's rise in the late forties and early fifties was paralleled by dramatic changes that occurred at approximately the same time among the working class. Whether there is any precise relationship between the advent of television and the changes within this population group is not well known, though it is fairly safe to assume that each was related to and influenced the other. The wage-earning class of Americans acquired greater job stability, more leisure time, more income and discretionary purchasing power. During the same period, working-class people began to buy their own homes in much larger numbers than before and to develop their own suburban communities. They also began to find for themselves and to purchase what was for them a new and diverse line of household and personal products. They became an important, distinctive, and accessible market, and television was perhaps partly instrumental in this development; it certainly was a mechanism by which these people were reached.

The most obvious changes in the working class involved the objects they now own, and these have had the effect of making these people appear more like the middle class. Behavior and styles of living, beliefs and values, also changed in the same direction but not to the same degree, so that the working class remains more than merely an occupational category in American social life. It still reflects a mode of living and an organization of personality that differs from middle-class values, aspirations, goals, and ways of acting. And it is on this basis that many of the different uses of and attitudes toward television among these population groups persist.

The working-class family in the child-rearing and homemaking years, when the age of the parents ranges between twenty and fifty, deals with television as a member of the family. Parents as well as children accept it fully. It is relied on for many gratifications, and it is used by all family members (both separately and together) in many ways and at many times. In their own view, if not by any objective measure, the set seems to be on hour after hour, and someone is likely to be watching it (or at least listening to it) most of this time. In the morning hours it will be the children, during the day it will be the mother. If there are children of preschool age they may be put in front of the set during the day so the mother won't be bothered by them. After school it will be the children again, and in the evening it will be the father, the adolescent boys and girls in the household, and, as time permits, the mother, too. The goal at most times and for most of these people is pleasure and enjoyment. They especially appreciate easygoing, relatively simple stimulation, provided that there is enough movement and activity to hold their attention and interest. Their demands

are typically modest, but their enthusiasm and enjoyment
are considerable.

Television for them, at its best, means a program with
known performers who seem to be talented and friendly
people. Themes and story lines should not be complicated or unnecessarily taxing on the intellect or the emotions. Working-class people will often describe their favorite programs and performers—and they have many of
each—in this manner:

> James Arness in *Gunsmoke*, he's a really good cowboy. Good
> actor too. I guess he's about the only good guy who stops in
> and drinks a beer or so. I like that Chester too. My kids really
> go for him. In fact, the whole family really likes him. I can't
> say that I would like to see more of him, once a week is fine;
> but I would sure hate to see less of him. . . . Lucille Ball, she's
> different, kind of screwified. Her show is a riot. She's kind of
> like a dizzy blond but there is a little something more there.
> I feel her program would appeal to all ages too. I'd like to see
> more of her.

In comedy shows, this audience wants "a good laugh."
In drama, it wants obvious themes and unmistakable
high points and resolutions. In family-situation programs,
it wants reality, even if this reality is obviously exaggerated. In variety shows, it wants variety; too much of the
same thing, and sometimes too much of the same show,
becomes monotonous. In stories of all types, the working-class audience wants clearly defined roles, without
too many subtle or psychological complications. Panel
and quiz programs should be sharply done, dramatic,
with impressively knowledgeable participants whose intelligence leans heavily in the direction of good memory
and facility in verbalizing. Westerns are expected to show
a world in which men are men and women are women,
and, as in detective stories and mysteries, action must
dominate. Aggression, violence, and sex are not necessarily interpreted as disruptive but merely as a part of
the program's world. They are not shocking but vicarious-

ly affirmative, to be directly enjoyed. "That's it, give it to him; he got him!"

These and similar qualities reflect the kinds of people composing the working-class audience, the ways in which they see life and the ways in which they see themselves. They are not reflective people; neither are they very tolerant of complicated activities of an intellectual or emotional sort. The world, to their way of thinking, is or is supposed to be well organized into regular, stable, recognizable categories. Pleasure should be pleasure, sorrow should be sorrow, and they do not readily accept complex mixtures of these qualities. Their inclination is to respond impulsively, and they expect television to be of much the same order. Its people should be friendly, and performers whom they suspect to be "phony" are likely to be rejected.

Television for these people functions as a readily available companion and activity—a thing to do—in a world in which there are not too many alternatives. It does not compete for their time with other activities as it is likely to do with middle-class audiences. Working-class viewers are inclined to take what comes, and TV suits their inclination well. It also suits many of their interpersonal needs, as something for the family to do together, as a focal point for keeping the members at home, as something to talk about with one another. It becomes an object in the family setting about which husbands and fathers (and sometimes mothers and older brothers and sisters) can exercise their authority when they decide what programs will be watched and how long the kids can stay up. In these families TV is recognized as giving information about the world that otherwise might not be acquired, and, in a similar way, it provides resource material for more personal activities and fantasies.

Whatever problems TV seems to present regarding its effect on children, among these viewers it is found to be useful and sensible. A few of the functions it serves are these:

It reinforces parental authority by showing specific ways for adults and children to behave, while also setting forth worthwhile models (as in Father Knows Best, Lassie, Captain Kangaroo, *and* Disneyland).

It gives children something to do besides fighting with each other, thereby cutting down on family tensions.

It is a cheap and easily available baby sitter; since it is a present attraction and stimulation for children, it thereby frees the parents for pursuing their own interests.

It teaches children about the modern world and what is current.

It is like an adjunct to school, providing intellectual content, and it teaches children about life, feelings, relations, people. It is a life experience and an accessory to parents.

It provides worthwhile and enjoyable entertainment for children, with fun, humor, and some meaningful imaginative material.

Very often television is used as a "weapon" for controlling and rewarding children. As one working-class mother put it:

I let the kids watch just one half-hour of killing every night, and that's all! They try to get me to let them see more, but if they disobey me and put it on when I tell them not to, I just take the set into my bedroom and it doesn't come out for a couple of days. One half-hour of killing is enough!

Working-class parents, like others, are concerned with the specific content of programs and may be apprehensive of the violent self-expressiveness that may be aroused in their children. On the whole, however, they appreciate what television offers them as parents and what it offers their children. A temptation to restrict viewing, for the kids and for themselves, comes to mind now and then, but implementing such a restriction is difficult and seems "unreasonable," and most such attempts fall by the way. The parents and the children both give in to this enticing activity, and they usually end up watching their sets a great deal, often at random (except perhaps for a few regular favorites). Thus, the stereotype of the television fan fits the working-class viewer more than others, as less motivated to act in an energetic, censoring, or selective fashion.

This attitude is not to be confused with the stereotype of the "overly embracing" position, the viewer hypnotized by television and completely indiscriminate in his tastes, standards, and program choices. Neither should it hide the fact that among this audience television is perceived as a dynamic, changing thing, and that these viewers, too, have gradually modified their attitudes toward it. As one woman pointed out:

> Five years ago television fascinated me and I watched everything. I also had more time to watch as I only had three children. But maybe I am more selective now regarding programs. I used to love to watch *I Love Lucy*. I also liked Milton Berle, Sid Caesar, and even Arthur Godfrey and Julius LaRosa. I do watch TV less now and I don't think the stars are as big today as they were then. I know I spent much more time watching TV and I looked forward to it every night. Now it's more of a hit or miss thing; if you are at home you watch it.

This woman was then asked, "What do you think television will be like five years from now?" She replied:

> Well, I hope it won't be all atomic energy and bombs. I think there will be more educational programs and more programs on current events. There will be more courses on TV for which you will be able to receive credit. School teachers are able to take courses on TV and receive credit for them now. They have language courses for credit and the TV may be used to help people who cannot attend formal classes in school.
>
> I don't think that the other programs will change too much. They will have to have programs that interest children, teenagers, and adults, separately and together in groups.
>
> The men will continue to like sports programs and they will continue to hate live plays. I hope I don't get sick of the soap operas, though I don't think TV will be that different five years from now. Maybe instead of cowboys we will have Milton Berle back and his old jokes will sound new again. The TV studios may run out of Indians and sheriffs and I'll be glad when they do.

Her idealized hope, like that of others in this large audience group, is that television will be a force for good.
For aspiring working- and middle-class people this goal is
symbolized as "education." But a more realistic appraisal
also makes her reflect that television needs to have things
for all kinds of people and that, when you come right
down to it, men will continue to like sports and dislike
live plays, and women (like herself) will want their soap
operas. Maybe it really won't be so very different, she
wishes implicitly. In fact, maybe it should be what it used
to be, when we laughed at Milton Berle's jokes. Maybe
it should just continue to be as gratifying and as pleasant
as it was in the past and, in many ways, still is—a wish
widely subscribed to by this audience of television embracers.

The Homebound Young: Children to Twelve Years

If there is anything that may be said to characterize
childhood, it is development, growth, and intensive learning. A child must learn many things: to master the growth
that biology dictates, to learn about the social and natural world he lives in, to know what is expected of him
by this world, to understand his capacities and where he
fits into the scheme of things. He must do these things
both in the present, in his role of child, and looking ahead
into adulthood.

In this busiest period of growth in the human cycle almost anything is grist for the child's mill, both in his learning and in his mastery of what is learned. It thus seems
appropriate and natural to children (and sometimes to
adults) that television is an added resource in learning
about life.

Television serves many functions throughout childhood,
and different uses and meanings come to the fore at different stages of development. Sex, social class, parental
attitudes, familial styles of living, all have some influence,

and the interrelationship among these is often complex. However, the main reaction of children up to the age of adolescence is one of close identification with and considerable use of TV. They see it simply as a generally available object in the home with which to spend time, one that is always interesting and diverting.

For young children up to the age of nine or so, television is a "fun box" that never seems to run out of different things to offer. With its movement, words, and thematic content, it is a strange kind of thing that seems somewhere between the animate (a person) and the inanimate (a toy). People, animals, and cartoon figures appear, but the child cannot touch them or make them respond to him in reality. Though the child can manipulate the set like a toy by switching channels, his physical role is essentially passive. His main interest is in the stimulation the various elements offer on the level of fantasy.

Children, and especially those of preschool age, respond to the pictures and sounds of television as if someone is there to attend to their needs—to tell a story, to be with them, to amuse them, and (in some respects most important of all) to provide a focus of attention and thus to keep them occupied. Often parents and other important adults are busy tending to other family members, chores, or their own concerns, and the child feels he would like the companionship and attention of an adult. Television often serves this function, with people like Miss Frances, Captain Kangaroo, and Frazier Thomas. Comedians, too, when children understand their antics and humor, as well as cartoons with some of the animals and characters in toy-like form, are easily understood, stimulating, and fun.

Certain characters and people in the programs become special kinds of "friends," somewhat in the same manner as children create makebelieve playmates for enjoyment, learning, and testing out ideas and behavior. But by the

age of six or seven, with more frequent and regular contacts with other children in kindergarten and grade
school, such special "private attachments" begin to fade.
It is at this time that the need for direct relationships with
real playmates becomes more important and continues
so through the school years.

During the child's school years the daily routine becomes more highly organized, and television comes to be
only one of many activities available. It is at this time that
it becomes defined as "something to do." A six-year-old
girl describes it in this way:

> I go to school, and I like recess and singing. Then I come
> home for lunch and watch TV. Then I go to school. I play
> after school an(watch TV.

Television also becomes a good in-between activity for
children of six to twelve. It is watched between school
and play, while waiting for lunch, before breakfast, after
school, and before dinner. It fills up time spaces and it
breaks up the more dominant activities of school, play,
and family time. In doing so, it becomes, in fact, a very
important aspect of a child's life. When children want to
be by themselves and away from the unwanted stimulation of adults or other children—or when they want to be
distracted from inner tensions, and thus away from themselves—they retreat to the television set. (This is also a
common adult use of television, though one that finds more
frequent expression among those who embrace it than
among others.) TV sound, action, and activity form a
screen against the impinging world, be it external or in-
ternal. The emphasis here may be on complete absorption with the program or it may be primarily on one's self,
with the ongoing program functioning mainly to stimulate feelings and thoughts about one's own private world.
Inner-directed viewing of this sort tends to take place after
a strenuous period of activity or high stimulation. It is
used, by children and also by adults, in an attempt to

comfort themselves from hurt, either self-inflicted or otherwise.

When the child begins school, the "embracing" qualities exemplified by this audience come increasingly to the fore. Viewing frequency increases, and television becomes a prominent home activity, something that is done at set times, on a regular basis, in routine ways. Familiarity with a wide range of programs increases, and performers and programs become more sharply defined. There is more awareness at this age that television entertains, and this stimulation becomes a prime motivation for tuning in and watching. Preferences take shape and govern what is watched and what is not, though they have less influence on the times when television is watched. Generalized standards for evaluation begin to form and play a significant role in how the child responds to what he sees. It is also during these years that parents begin to worry most actively about the influence television has on their children, and contributing to this concern is the amount of time the young ones spend watching the set, the intensity of their involvement with what they see, and the obvious sense of enjoyment they are likely to show.

Our interviews with children reveal that there are many important inducements drawing the child to the set, which are the substance of the relationship between the child viewer and television content. For example, television propounds social realities to children and in this way serves as a great socializer, an adjunct to parents in presenting the world as it is perceived by parents and, more generally, by adults. The fact that so much of what children watch is also watched by adults contributes to this meaning. Beyond the entertainment, pretense, and fantasy of the medium is a representation of the "real" world. Children know this and respond to it as an authoritative source of what is real and current in our culture.

TV presents children with models of the "ideal" family. Family shows and family situations as portrayed on television inform youngsters of what is expected and approved in behavior, and they are quick to catch any inferences to be drawn about children from more "adult" shows.

Television is also important in helping children understand and master their own life experience, just as play represents an attempt at mastery of learning. Children respond to meaningful symbolic content. By vicariously identifying with the action and the characters he sees, a child can safely express affection, discharge hostility, play at being what he wants—while learning what he and the world are like.

From the child's point of view, television teaches parents certain important things. Children enjoy watching with their family the programs that expose and point up the needs, likes, and tastes of children, including themselves. In this way, wants and behavior patterns as well as desirable products become known, justified, and legitimized.

In terms of programs, children aged six to ten tend regularly to watch "their own" programs. They are less involved in what is available to them by the choices of other family members. They like best the various cartoon programs, like *Mickey Mouse* and *Popeye* or *Heckle and Jeckle*. They enjoy the stories, such as *Tom Terrific* and *Crusader Rabbit,* and like the combination of animal, cartoon, and humorous interests in *Huckleberry Hound. Captain Kangaroo* stands out as one of the most beloved programs, both for children and for parents. Comedians and comic family situations are meaningful and fun; children can be delighted by the childishness of a reassuring adult.

They are stimulated by the Three Stooges and Dennis the Menace, the former because of the abundance of slapstick, movement, and silliness, the latter because Den-

nis does what they would often like to do. (Parents typically disapprove of both these shows because of the "bad
example" they set for the youngsters.) *Disneyland* seems
outstanding because it teaches them about the world.
They enjoy watching such shows as *Father Knows Best,
Peter and the Wolf*, and *Lassie* primarily because there is
a solid plot line that sharply integrates the show for them
and makes it easy to follow. They enjoy other shows that
have a focus for their attention, with movement or specific dramatic events, such as jugglers, tightrope walkers,
clowns, animals, and dancers.

Children are often attracted to but are frightened by
many adult programs, such as detective shows. Often they
will sense and respond to the demanding, sinister, unrelieved overtones with mixed feelings, much uncertainty,
but a persistent fascination at the revelation of what
adulthood may really be like.

The ages of ten through thirteen are likely to bring
changes in how television is used and in what it means
to children. On the one hand, with the increase of adult
demands, school work, and peer-group pressures, television takes on a special and undemanding meaning. Children enjoy it, can relax and daydream with it, and thus
begin to hold it out as a reward for themselves. Parents
strongly reinforce this by limiting and circumscribing their
viewing. At the same time, these are the preadolescent
years, and children of this age, depending on their physical and social maturity, are beginning to break away from
earlier attitudes and behaviors. Here, then, is a period of
transition, when the intense involvement of the embracing attitude gradually diminishes to the more purposeful
and selective viewing that distinguishes it from the accommodating and protesting attitudes toward television.

Preadolescent children want and need ways in which
to relate to other children, and the content of television becomes more actively a form of social currency.

The solitary gratifications may still remain and may be primary in attracting the viewer, but television at this period of life and with this audience group becomes a substance around which social relations develop and maintain themselves. The content, stars, and stories of television help them find mutual interests and focus on their own similarities and differences. TV is discussed, and it is a way of relating to others—both family and friends. It can stimulate relationships when a program is viewed together with other persons, hence affording mutual interests and enjoyment. At the same time, it also provides an opportunity for diminishing overt contacts and interactions, since a family unit or a few friends can watch together but need not actively relate to each other. A passive presence is often quite sufficient.

Television is used to consolidate the gains and satisfactions of earlier childhood. Programing classified as "childish" continues to have an appeal for this age group. They still enjoy *Captain Kangaroo* and cartoons, though protesting they watch such programs "over the shoulder" of a younger sister or brother or only occasionally, "by chance." But at this late childhood age the status of television as an authoritative source of adult reality also becomes more important. It is the easiest and most enjoyable method of keeping informed on what is current, whether this be products, commercials, stars, personalities, shows, events, or ideas.

Preadolescent children watch a greater variety of shows, including "bang-bangs" of the Western or detective type. They are impressed by the relatively forbidden shows that are considered adult or appear after their bedtime. This is especially true for shows that adults think should be for adults. These are programs that children think are enjoyable, too, such as *The Untouchables* and *77 Sunset Strip*. Comedy of all sorts is enjoyed, including old-style slapstick, zany characters, family situations, plays on words, etc. There is an increasing interest in powerful, well-integrated dramatic shows, particularly on the part of girls. Boys tend to enjoy adventure stories and heroics. Girls and some boys of this age enjoy "teen-age" dancing shows, like Dick Clark's, while boys begin to make sports their special interest.

Highly moralistic stories, either Westerns or dramas, that are unrelieved by humor and seem too adult, serious, and demanding of good behavior are not always liked. These preadolescents have outgrown the sweet and simple animal vignettes of early childhood. And variety shows are watched only in part for favorite stars and people, but otherwise are considered dull, repetitious, and "goofy."

CHAPTER FOUR

TELEVISION
PROTESTED

The embrace of television, as described in the previous chapter, is not highly vocal. Its occurrence in our society is expressed in the act of watching television and in occasional letters to program booklets. Much more apparent on the American scene are the protests and criticisms levied against the medium. These negative attitudes are able to achieve their more manifest expression because, being protests, they carry more energy toward being heard. Also, they are attitudes held most prominently by people who have the voice and influence to gain access to magazines, newspapers, and conferences. Third, they are given this access because television is considered a legitimate object of critical review. Outbursts against the medium are more newsworthy than is praise, making it difficult to distinguish how much of their public visibility is due to the fact that newspapers and magazines are in competition with television.

These are various factors that exaggerate the sense of protest perceived against television, making acceptance private and protest public. This amplification of criticism forces many people to conform and to express the public view that excessive violence should be controlled on television; and even survey results may be presented in a way that inflates the sound of protest. For example, the

June 14, 1961, release of the American Institute of Public Opinion (the Gallup Poll) was headed "Greater Curbs on TV Programs Called for by Many Americans." The subhead was "Study Finds More Want Curbs on TV, Radio Than on Press; Violence on TV Cited Often." The tabular results are presented to emphasize the findings that 49 per cent of the persons interviewed approve of placing greater curbs or controls on the programs presented by television and radio and that 57 per cent of the persons favoring greater curbs cited excessive violence in justification of their views. While this may be factually correct, the method of presentation obscures the fact that actually only 28 per cent of the total sample is protesting excessive violence, a distinct minority that in many surveys would be brushed aside rather than given headline prominence. Similarly, the group protesting "programs harmful to children" is only 14 per cent of the total sample; the group protesting "immorality, sex" is only 8 per cent; the group protesting "commercials" (false ads, too many ads) is only 6 per cent—and many of these protesters are the same people, citing more than one area where they would favor curbs. Actually, a larger percentage of the total sample (16 per cent) protests the intransigence of newspapers, desiring curbs on "defense information helpful to the enemy," than complains about television programs harmful to children.

The point is not that television does not provide cause for complaint or that there are not many Americans who view it critically, but that it seems useful to put into sociological perspective the fact that the protesting attitude is a limited one. It goes along with certain views of modern life and is not merely the objective diagnosis of a manifest evil. Clearly, some viewers are more restless than others.

The Characteristics of Protest

The protests against television derive from a variety of sources. They may come from a parent who is especially concerned about child-rearing; they may be directed at television as an art form failing to realize its potentialities; they may view the medium as an instrument for social influence that is being misused; and so on. These negative views are usually part of some general definition of television, involving considerations of the kind of object it is, what its purposes should be, and how it should and should not be used.

To people who characteristically criticize television, the set has an anomalous status as an object in the home. Typically, they would like to look upon it as merely an appliance, something not unlike a telephone or a dishwasher. Seen in this light, it is essentially utilitarian rather than pleasurable. It belongs because it is a modern artifact, a substantial thing manufactured in our society that a consumer is likely to have in a fully furnished home.

The extreme critic may go so far as to despise television and all that it stands for and refuse to admit it to the house. Such a person is, by and large, the last holdout, a purist in the attitude of protest. Even he himself may wonder if he is not alienating himself too much from his culture. One such man, bothered by his children's devotion to TV and all that this implied to him, irritatedly gave his set to his janitor. He has since felt the need to rent a set during political campaigns, and he occasionally wonders whether there might not be enough "good things" on television (shows that his respected friends admire) to warrant having a set again.

An appliance of this sort is not expected to occupy a central place in the household. Usually it is somewhere to the side or in a room defined as relatively frivolous (den, family room, playroom, basement, child's room).

Often there is strong resistance to having the set in the living room or dining room—although these are honored sites in the homes of people who love television. Having the set in a less conspicuous place means that less significance is given to it, that it is used only when needed, thereby demonstrating one's aloofness and freedom from addiction. Attendance at the set is in itself affected by a less central location. People in the home are less likely to fall into casual watching, since going to the set is an act of choice; it is not on prominent view and therefore not so easily available.

Sometimes uneven attendance is accompanied by rather sharply distorted knowledge of what is available on television. The most ardent protester is likely to divide program content into two distinct categories. Near to him are those things to which he is willing to give attention—sometimes even addiction. Then, across a gap of unawareness that includes a large body of program material, he sees those shows or performers that stand out as symbolic of the terrible faults of the medium.

Many of the people who protest television do not differ in their patterns of watching from those who view it in a more receptive way. They show familiarity with the same range of programs, can identify the customary television performers, and like some of the shows that find general favor. In these respects there is a large amount of overlap among viewers. Protest and criticism often come as hindsight, more as a matter of guilt over having slipped, having lost self-discipline, than one of actually avoiding the set in the first place. The difference, then, between many protesters and many embracers of television is in intensity of attitudes, in emphasis on different values, and in what television watching means to them.

An antagonistic attitude toward television does not preclude some specific program addictions. Intense preferences may fall among the kinds of shows that are ordinar-

ily criticized, the specific instance being excused on one
ground or another as an allowable lapse. At times, the
relatively less visible location of the television set permits some secret indulgence, as though not watching "in
public" were more permissible.

In general, television does tend to play a smaller role
in the life of the protester. Such a person might watch
about one-fourth as much as an avid viewer, being more
likely to read, do things around the house, visit, do homework (whether school or office), engage in hobby and
family activities, etc. These other interests are valued as
things that should not be ignored in favor of television.
They are regarded as very important parts of a successful and satisfying life, and absorption in television is seen
as antagonistic to these values.

To understand more clearly this view of television, it
will be helpful to examine the personal and social aims
protesters are likely to cherish and to see how these relate to their definitions of television. A foremost goal is
learning. These people tend to emphasize the importance
of acquiring information, knowledge, and understanding.
This aim is highly ramified, with consequences both for
children and for adults. For children, it means that television should not distract them from academic learning
by reducing their time and incentive for reading and
study, and when they do attend to television it should
provide them with experiences that are educational. One
mother talked about controlling her children in this way:

> I have lots to say about the children's TV habits. The
> two younger children will watch providing someone older is
> watching with them. They are four and two years old. They
> do not watch regularly. They like cartoons if they watch, also
> Laurel and Hardy and the Three Stooges. But I stopped that.
> . . . The most avid watcher is the oldest boy; he's nine and a
> half. He used to watch every Saturday morning, all morning,
> but now he goes to the "Y." He watched after supper, but
> now with daylight saving time he goes out to play. He likes

cartoons, and my husband gets upset over that. He likes all cowboys, and he's now beginning to like comedians . . . . I limit the time they spend watching, but not the programs. I have finally controlled the watching by finding other things for them to do. I don't let them watch before dinner. Neither of the two older children are readers, which I blame on television. At one point they would wake up at 5 or 6 A.M. to watch Laurel and Hardy and they would be in a trance from it all day. But we stopped that.

What's my opinion of children's TV? There is not enough educational TV on at the right hours. They loved big productions, like *Peter Pan* or *The Wizard of Oz*. They still talk about them. I tried to get them to watch *I've Been Reading*, but I couldn't . . . . I'm very glad this excessive, almost slavish, attitude has stopped. I don't see where they have learned anything from it. I haven't seen anything good from it. They see killing, they see brutality, but they have had no bad effects from it either. It has killed their reading though. Well, enough of the children . . . .

What children want to watch is often not what their parents want them to watch, and only the most ardent protesters feel sufficiently able and motivated to control their children's viewing habits. Such parents usually have narrower conceptions of what constitutes educational experience than do those who are more casual about television. The latter will like to believe that all television is educational for children, that they learn many things from it, even when such learning is not the purpose of the program. Protesting parents do not deny that this may happen, but they are vigorous in wanting learning to go on within the framework of more formally defined teaching procedures. They are therefore more inclined toward special educational channels and toward programs whose aim is clearly to instruct children about the nature of the world.

For adults themselves, a focus on learning tends to refer to the acquisition of current information. They define television especially in terms of its ability to bring the outside world to one's home, carrying facts, explanations, and realism. The goal of television should be to widen the individual's horizon, to assist him in understanding the modern world, how it is functioning, and what it requires by way of an informed public. To the protester, television should be, and is insufficiently, a facility for being *knowing*, whether through being generally educated or specifically informed:

> I think there should be more educational programs, and eventually I hope that will be the trend. I think it will be used more in schools as teaching aids. It's not the best way to teach, but it is necessary. The children absorb a lot, like from the programs they have on Sunday afternoon. They should have the more educational type of thing, like plays and operas, although that last opera I saw on television was so messed up it disgusted you. I don't know if all this will happen, but it is what I would like to have happen.

These desirable functions of television define it less as a family member, welcome guest, or entertainer, as other people tend to see it. Rather, it should be a messenger, representing the outside world, bringing news of the day and the atmosphere of immediate events. Beyond this, at a higher level of intellectual stimulation, television should be like a Greek chorus, giving comment and consideration, pro and con, dealing with important issues of the times—political, sociological, health, etc.

Other major areas of concern to television protesters grow out of values relating to improvement. They believe that people should make active efforts to improve themselves and to move their children toward personality growth and enhancement. The development of skills in problem-solving described above is part of this view. Of great importance also is a devotion to cultural uplift. Critics believe that television is deficient in its effect on public taste. A typical statement of this attitude was expressed by Leroy Collins, president of the National Association of Broadcasters before a Senate subcommittee on June 19, 1961: "Crime and violence in present television programming (are) unnecessary and undeserving of broadcast." There is not enough scientific evidence to prove that this causes juvenile delinquency, he added, "but this gives no justification for the use of violence merely for the sake of violence. To the contrary, such is offensive to simple good taste, seriously downgrades the television art and should be eliminated." It is characteristic of protesters to believe that they have and can recognize "good taste"; the average citizen does not normally define his capacity for discrimination in these terms.

A desire for artistic and esthetic enlargement is not necessarily prevalent among protesters, but it is characteristic of certain types within this group. These people are interested in increasing the amount of television time given to classical performances, to concerts, ballet, and the elevated dramatic arts. They distinguish between sensual, violent actions for their own sake and their employment as realistic elements in significant drama.

More general among protesters is a concern with moral uplift. They often deride exaggerated esthetic interests as an excuse for sexual or aggressive content and advocate "wholesomenesss." The general attitude that television should have programs that are "good for children" is often a moral preoccupation. A majority of people, not only ardent television protesters, would like improvement in this realm. Many mothers not otherwise antagonistic to television think the Three Stooges are a grotesque example for children, and fret about the susceptibility of their youngsters to being excited by television and to imitate poor models of speech and behavior. At times, people who protest television more vigorously seem to find almost no offsetting experiences available on the screen.

In addition to intellectual, cultural, and moral improvement, another aspect of the attitude of protest has to do with interpersonal relations. Television is criticized for its interference with social skills and activities. A common complaint is that watching tends to replace conversation, that rather than bring the family together it isolates the members from each other. Television is regarded as passive behavior that cuts down doing things with and for other people. Protesters are likely to include people who value social relations, who stress the importance of dealing with people to achieve personal fulfillment as well as vocational success.

At a more personal level, there is a belief that television interferes with personality development, that it has deleterious effects on behavior, producing poor eating or sleeping habits, diminishing self-control, supplanting self-expression and individuality with conformity and stereotypical thinking—or, as some would have it, no thinking at all:

> One has to think very little to enjoy most programs. It could act as a substitute for thinking; you could become stagnated and then your life enters a humdrum sort of thing. It could become like cards, just something to pass the time away. Life is too short to do that.

Protesters look down on the level and caliber of most television content as appealing to the lowest common denominator in a mass society. They believe that bad appeals drive out good, that children will naturally prefer to watch the Three Stooges rather than *Captain Kangaroo, The Untouchables* rather than Shirley Temple. They feel not only that television fails sufficiently to play the roles of messenger, Greek chorus, uplifter, teacher, and the like, but that it is frighteningly attractive, that it is an intruder, a seducer, an opiate. (Some protesters like television this way, saying that if it got any better, they would be tempted to watch it too much.)

Since television's presentations tend to fit into the value scheme and esthetic preferences of what protesters judge to be debased, mass mediocrity, they struggle with the problem of how to improve the situation. Often they have no solution beyond a wish that television would become more "educational." There are three ways in which protesters commonly seek to attain this goal. One is for parents to influence television content by complaining about the programs offered. There is some recognition that this does not always work, since a majority of people can seldom be prevailed upon to act in this way. But it has the advantage of being a democratic position that helps ward off charges of intended censorship, and it keeps program offerings in line with "what viewers want."

A second avenue for seeking improvement, and one that tends to be more closely identified with professional protesters who are associated with the broadcasting industry, is for the networks to take action in using "simple good taste" in TV programing. Sponsors will continue to be guided by ratings, this view holds, and therefore networks should be freed from the censoring control of advertisers and exert their own more enlightened and esthetic preferences. A third view maintains that nothing will work short of government intervention, either to insulate the advertiser from programing decisions or, more drastically, to determine how many hours are to be allotted to discussion programs, educational series, detective stories, concerts, Westerns, and so on. But this remains a minority view, even among protesters.

In summary, the views that protesters have of television give their attitude a special flavor. They believe television should convey more realism than it does (and they look down on giveaway shows that seem especially false to life). They think that the entertainment and relaxation that the medium provides should be nonsentimental (making variety shows and plays superior to Westerns and comedies). They are disdainful of soap operas and melodramas as insipid and nonrevelatory. They are likely to have more interest in seeing real people on television than performers, and among performers they prefer people they consider to be "real actors" rather than "TV personalities."

The Protesters of Television

Among the people who protest television are several subgroups with different reasons for and different emphases in their views. Some protest verbally but not behaviorally; others complain and watch little; others do not complain but do not watch very much either.

Protest from the Middle Class

Protest is by and large an upper-status, middle-class phenomenon. Upper-middle-class people are particularly given to criticizing television, to noting its shortcomings, and to wishing for improvement in it. They are less likely to watch whatever shows up on their screens, or, if they do, they feel very unhappy with themselves for doing so. One upper-middle-class woman offers typical protests while describing a great amount of television watching. She comments:

> I'm ashamed to say I watch television that much. The caliber of the programs is not up high; it's a waste of time. But I can't help it. I don't know why I watch some of those sub-caliber programs. Sometimes I turn it off, but it's easier to just leave it on, even when you watch horrible ones, like those Westerns . . . . Some are intelligent and worthwhile, but the rest are about horses and cattle and plain junk . . . . As for the effect on the family, television is killing conversation. But we are making an effort to cut down on it.

Ordinarily, the upper-middle-class approach to television is more active and self-directing. Selection, discrimination, and planning are the keynotes of their viewing. That is, there must be a sense of explicit and meritorious rationale about a choice to watch particular shows, accompanied by open criticism and strongly formulated intellectual opinions.

The upper-middle-class person's style of life is typically bound up with a great deal of activity, at home, socially, and organizationally. Even his day-to-day, normal social contacts are "busy," and all his activities tend to be organized and planned. Explicitness, thinking, verbal expression, the weighing of alternatives, all these are applied in the pursuit of an active and determined choice. Applied to television, this makes the upper-middle-class person deliberative, detached, and impatient. It also means that some control in viewing is exercised, both in how much time is spent and in what is watched, and not much room is left for self-indulgence. The controls are firmly set, and there is general apprehension that they may be (even if only rarely) transgressed.

Upper-middle-class people tend to single out particular types of programs. Although they believe that some programs are worthwhile, the range seems too limited to them. And because often they watch only certain things that fall within this narrow range, they are prone to fatigue and satiation through the monotony of their own choices.

Socially mobile middle-class viewers—those who are in the process of bettering their social position—also tend to think of themselves as selective viewers who plan what they watch, see what is worthwhile, and control their time efficiently in an effort to match inner needs and outer reality. The process of planning appears to cut down on the indulgent aspects of viewing through the exercise of choice and the imposition of controls. These mobile people want not only to be "virtuous" by exercising self-control but to be active and constructive in relation to what they see. They want to use what they watch as a way of testing out their aspirations, of learning something that will broaden and help them in their strivings for social improvement and a better, more desirable way of life.

A main difficulty that mobile middle-class people encounter is that much of what appears on television seems to be entertaining rather than educational. This, expressed as a criticism, often means that the content is felt to be too stimulating, sensuous, and provocative. They are afraid to give in to the temptations offered, to lose control and sight of their goals.

The In-between Teen-Agers

In our studies, teen-agers generally feel relatively alienated from television. While they are not serious or strong critics, they have mixed attitudes about what it does or means to them. They can become devoted and enthusiastic fans of certain TV personalities or one or another specific show, but generally they and the medium are not in notable rapport, since they feel that it addresses itself mainly to young children and to established families.

The transition between childhood and adulthood is difficult for most youngsters. It is a period of growing away from home and family or becoming a daughter or a son rather than a child, of consolidating a unique identity as a human being. Peer-group pressures are at their peak; it is important to have friends, to be liked, and to be one's own man (or woman). These youngsters have a high level of energy, with almost constant activity in high-pitched sociability; in keeping up with ever larger amounts of homework, responsibilities, and preoccupations; with improving and discovering themselves.

Television, besides being difficult to manage in terms of time—where does it fit into all this activity?—is problematic on a deeper level. It is part of the home and is identified with home and family life. But family relations tend to be most difficult and tense for the teenager and his parents, and television often becomes a focus of increased tension when teen-agers do become really absorbed in it. Attitudes toward TV shows during this period vary in intensity, depending on the degree of comfort and integration the adolescent can find within himself, his roles, and his position in the family environment.

Often, specific program content—especially when it includes sex, violence, and complex interpersonal relationships—while both attractive and repellent, heightens the adolescent's self-consciousness and his struggle for growth, maturity, and identity.

Adolescents strive toward achieving an identity by emulating public personalities in two ways, both of which find support in television. They attempt to identify with and take for their own the qualities and traits that are highly valued. They may also experiment with "negative identity," that is, they may emulate the worst qualities of "bad people" in an effort to master the badness in themselves. This may show itself in dancing styles, experiments with extreme dress or makeup, or absorption in the fantasy of *77 Sunset Strip's* glamour.

The adolescent seriously experiments with roles learned on TV, while satirizing and parodying many of the values expressed in these roles. Commercials, drama, stars, stories, and format are ridiculed in an effort to test the established values and find identities.

There is in all this a kind of search for truth, since most teen-agers feel their parents to be no longer the source of the only and full truth. They feel the need to go beyond, to branch out. They need "facts" to be able to assert themselves as adults. They need to keep up with what's going on, to be able to participate in the peer-group culture. This includes being aware of current TV heroes—Dick Clark, Doug McClure, and the others.

It is also at this age that sex differences in attitudes toward television begin to stabilize. The boys enjoy the masculine, the far-out, and the violent, as depicted in Westerns, detective and crime shows, sports, adventure stories, and mysteries. The girls feel much lesss comfortable with such strong emotions and behavior and prefer to stay with family shows, musicals, old movies, with some emphasis on drama and human relations. For both groups, the scientific, educational, and news programs hold some interest, stemming primarily from the orientation toward learning that is inculcated but often unsatisfied at school.

Parents as Protesters

All parents are likely to have views toward television that are governed mainly by their personalities, social class, status, age, and the like. However, since most parents are outdone in the adoration of television by their children, problems in their feelings and attitudes arise out of the fact of the parental relationship. Thus, in addition to seeing many merits in TV, most parents, including those who are otherwise not protesters, will show at least a streak of protest *as* parents.

Asking parents about television and children is tantamount to inquiring as to the state of the world and which way it is going. There are those who believe "it's going to the dogs," those who "don't know," those who think "things are getting better," and the "reasonable" confused majority. It is clear, however, that there is a grudging belief that television is a profound influence on today's children and on how they are going to grow.

All parents, regardless of social class or life style, address themselves first and foremost to the issue of television's formative influence and whether and to what extent it undermines parental authority, control, and the social and individual goals the parents set forth. Those who emphasize parental influence as most important in children's development (as opposed to school, peers, and church) are concerned about its undesirable (and some believe evil) competition in child-rearing. A second group, who see a multiplicity of forces shaping the child, are more accepting. A third group are those who think that there are certain basic tendencies that develop in the child regardless of who does what. They minimize personal, parental, school, and church influences and are most accepting of television, but they are a distinct minority.

Most parents have formulated a position encompassing positive as well as negative aspects. The protesting aspects have already been described; here they may be usefully summarized:

> *Television diminishes parental authority, providing undesirable content of violence and contrary morality.* The Untouchables, Hitchcock Presents, *horror movies, detective shows, and the like are instances.*
>
> *It provides bad examples, such as Dennis the Menace and the Three Stooges, who seem to have created a good many "menaces, according to the public.*
>
> *TV, by its symbolic content and sometimes its violent movement (even on children's shows), overstimulates children so that parents find handling them difficult.*
>
> *It creates family tensions by over-use, problems in selection, inability to hold children's attention—and parental disagreement on what is considered valuable for the child.*
>
> *It is a passive experience for children that does not give enough; it leaves them with few autonomous resources.*
>
> *It does not provide adequate intellectual stimulation.*
>
> *It distracts children and interferes with school work and other responsibilities.*
>
> *It sets up desires and wants that parents believe are inappropriate to children or are undesirable. It is frustrating in this sense to parents who are unable or unwilling to meet these wants—of a different way of life, certain products, etc.*

What would parents like to see in the future for television as it affects children? Some few suggest pay TV as a means of controlling more closely what is seen and heard by children, with some hope that "better quality" program exposure will come about through stricter control. But most parents hopefully believe that there will come to be more programs directed toward children, embodying fantasy, stimulation, charm, humor, entertainment, and a taste of childhood in its innocence and whimsy. Some of the programs that parents think would be good for children are the classics, like *Tom Sawyer, Huckle-*

berry Finn, My Friend Flicka, Robinson Crusoe, fairy tales, and so on. Some parents would like to see more family shows with palatable moral twists presented in a comic mode, to relieve their own tensions while serving as instructive entertainment for children. And almost all say that they would like more educational shows for children and believe that the growing ascendancy of science and scholarship that has been talked about so much will finally come to fruition in educational programing.

Intellectuals and Professionals as Vocal Critics

Prominent among the protesters are upper-middle-class people and those of marginal status who are also intellectuals, professionals of various kinds, social and artistic critics, etc. These are people who take a special stance in relation to television, one that is often quite distant or strongly geared to imposing a set of moral and esthetic values on other people. Their professional outlook and their intellectual position is one of protest and critical examination of the status quo. They take it as their task to object to conformity and the conventional taste of the majority. They include social scientists, newspaper columnists, writers, academic people and intellectuals in other occupations. Frequently they write articles or books, testify at hearings, and issue blasts at television at regular intervals. They include such individuals as David Susskind, John Fischer, Marya Mannes, John Crosby, Paul Molloy, Rod Serling, Joost Meerloo, Wilbur Schramm, Frederick Wertham, etc.

The different emphases these critics give to their protests are sometimes at odds. Some want freedom of expression and more classical elements of quality and theatricality, whereas others are plumping for moral values. As a result, for example, David Susskind may seek the dramatic license to depict scenes on television that Paul Molloy urges be put on late at night to protect children.

Some critics rock between the problems of freedom and control, uncertain how to achieve the superior television they would like without the imposed controls that might be required (how much censorship should the F.C.C. be empowered to exercise?). There are philosophic hazards in allowing democratic choice by the mass audience, as against placing the responsibility for an elevating choice on the networks or sponsors. John Fischer, of *Harper's Magazine,* appears to want more controls imposed on television than he would probably want to have interfering with his editorial judgment in running his magazine. Other people may work to find scientific evidence that television has damaging effects, and, when they cannot clearly prove this, they are inclined to fall back on their personal feelings and values, simply urging the improvement of an invaluable resource.*

*A recent example of this is found in the very interesting volume by Wilber Schramm, Jack Lyle, and Edwin B. Parker, TELEVISION IN THE LIVES OF OUR CHILDREN (Stanford, Calif.: Stanford University Press, 1961).

CHAPTER FIVE

TELEVISION ACCOMMODATED

The "accommodating" stance represents an attempt to balance several of the contending issues, strains, and gratifications associated with television, but clearly within a framework of acceptance. Television is viewed by these people as something wonderful and worthwhile even while they are cautious as to how it is used and suspicious of what it is and what it does. The stance itself falls between the two more extreme and distinctive attitudes and uses previously described. While it appears to share many of the praises and complaints of "television embraced" and "television protested," it nevertheless has its unique features.

The Characteristics of Accommodation

The accommodator is a person who likes and enjoys television. He accepts it as a major part of contemporary life, and he uses it as a significant part of his own life. He finds it difficult to think of himself and his present way of living without television, and he also is likely to be struck by the many differences its advent has meant for him, his family and friends, and the larger community. His attitude is that TV is a great thing; he is usually impressed by its past achievements and future responsibilities. Even its current offerings, though they frequently are criticized as not particularly good, provide him with a considerable ⸲ nount of acceptable and enjoyable entertainment.

> Television is one of the most important things in the world today, I guess. It's good for entertainment and it's good for bringing us the news and all the newest things that are happening. It's not as important to me as I think it might be to a lot of other people. I don't have too much time to watch it, but I guess I'd miss it if I couldn't turn it on when I want to. It's not the most important thing to my family, but they do enjoy it . . . . If there were less television available it wouldn't bother me if they would have it at night or on Sunday afternoon maybe. I don't get to look at it all day long like some people do and I don't think I would if I could. I would choose some good news programs and one or two good plays, and maybe a good musical show every week.

> I like TV myself. I don't criticize it, although some of the commercials are, oh, some are amusing, some good, and some not so good. There are so many good programs that they offset the bad ones. I think you can't have everything like you want in it, the way you want it. You can always change channels or cut it off.

> In general, I think TV is a very good medium. I don't know what I did without it before it came along. It gives you something to do, it's educational, it's exciting and relaxing . . .and if they could eliminate some of the rubbish that's on television, that would be fine.

Accommodators will spend a varying amount of time viewing television. On the average, they are likely to watch the set more than the protesters and less than the embracers, but the range is quite wide, from several hours a week to several hours a day. Much depends on individual circumstance, the other things the viewer does, and the mode of living developed in his particular household. Among these people television competes with other activities. It is not watched simply as a way of spending time; rather, it involves a a decision to watch and therefore a decision not to do something else—such as talking, household chores, working on hobbies, visiting, entertaining, going out, reading, and similar activities, which the accommodator sees as partly interchangeable with TV.

Though on occasion the accommodator may sit in front of his set mainly as a way of taking up time, he typically seeks out a particular program that he enjoys. He likes to keep up with his favorite series, spend an hour with a personality he's fond of, or relax with a light, easygoing situation comedy or a dramatic episode that he knows will be distracting and enjoyable. He usually anticipates what the program will be like and whether it will suit his particular needs and desires.

> We have a pretty set rule on what we watch, though sometimes there will be a special program and we'll watch that. We keep the TV guides from the newspaper where they have a listing of programs. Generally, in the daytime there are not many programs that I watch, and in the evening there are a few.

Selection and planning, then, are features of "television accommodated." This creates variability as to when television is watched in the same way that it makes for variation in how much time is spent in watching. Different nights of the week, for example, and different seasons of the year, too, will reflect greater variation among accommodators than among embracers. The embracer's viewing habits are likely to be more evenly distributed during the week and the seasons, but such is not likely to be the case for the accommodator, who determines his television viewing habits in relation to other activities.

Television, in the accomodating stance, is used for a variety of purposes and with a number of different goals in mind, but it provides entertainment, and this is by far the most significant meaning it has to these viewers. Their main goal in watching television is to derive enjoyment, and, since it is considered a wonderful way to relax, much of the viewing shapes itself around this goal.

Television informs and helps a person to be knowledgeable about current affairs, and among accommodators this usually has some special significance. "Education" and "culture" tend to be especially meaningful symbols for these people, and they feel that to be informed is a vital aspect of one's personality and social responsibilities. It is not surprising, then, that accommodators frequently speak of television in terms of how well it functions as an educative medium for children and for adults. This does not mean, however, that they want it to give great emphasis to this type of programing. They much prefer a diversity of content, a variety of entertainment, and the stimulating aspects of television that allow a person to enjoy it. Neither do they really want it to be very demanding, as occasionally they might suggest. Flexibility in how used and when watched, as well as in the functions it serves, is much more important to them.

Typically, accommodators have many favorite programs and stars. Television personalities come to be their good friends, and accommodators become sympathetic with their problems and are involved with their aspirations, successes, and failures. These viewers are able and eager to relate to television personalities and therefore make an effort to get to know who they are, what they are like, what is distinctive about them, and especially what personal gratifications they offer. They read about TV stars, talk about them with friends, and keep in touch with them as they appear on the screen. They also use these performers as personal models—to gain ideas and experiences, to pattern their own thoughts and behavior and attitudes, to make decisions regarding personal plans and social issues, to find solutions to individual and family problems, etc.

In general, the accommodator watches television in an intense manner. He is selective in what he watches, but what he selects he deals with in a conscientious way. He tends to stay with a series that is to his liking; his favorite performers will draw him to the set on a regular basis; if a particular program concept catches his fancy (such as a spectacular, a special kind of news analysis, or a certain type of dramatic presentation), he will plan to watch it as often as it is on. The accommodator's loyalty to programs and stars is such that he will stay with them over an extended period of time—*if* he continues to feel that they are living up to his expectations.

This is a subjective measure, sometimes spoken of as "good" television and defined only in vague and quite general ways, such as "the acting was very good," "it had to do with an important problem," "he was very funny," and so on. Underlying these evaluations is a feeling that the program, regardless of its specific type, content, or mode of presentation, reveals an effort to give something to the viewer. Themes that the viewer can identify with, a trace of sophistication and subtlety, a suggestion that the program is not only immediately enjoyable but that it has a more lasting quality—these appear to be associated with the accommodator's definition of "good" television. These people do not want to feel that watching is a waste of time—more pointedly, a waste of *their* time —and so long as the program or performers avoid being judged as trite, foolish, or unnecessary, they are generally acceptable. The accommodators' first inclination is to accept what television has to offer; in contrast to the protesters, they *want* to like television and have it suit their needs and tastes.

The accommodator wants *entertaining* television. This is largely a matter of feeling that the show is a "production," that it stimulates the viewer, that it holds him to the set and leaves him feeling that he has had a worthwhile experience. He also likes variety in his TV diet, both variety as to the different kinds of shows available to him (he is likely to watch all types) and variety within a single show or series. A diversity of emotions, themes, ideas, and people is most satisfactory; too much of the same thing strikes him as neither stimulating nor requiring his attention, and not as "good" television. He likes to think of himself as impatient with monotony and to believe that his tastes do not permit him to enjoy repetitive television. (A more realistic interpretation is that he is uncomfortable with programs of this kind, since they imply that he is merely watching for the sake of watching.)

Along with a general acceptance of television, the accommodating stance carries with it a variety of qualifications and suspicions and a sense of caution. In some respects, TV is all too wonderful, and the accommodator is fearful of being drawn in by this abundance of a good thing. How consciously this feeling is held varies a good deal, but, one way or another, either directly or implicitly, it is reflected in the attitudes and behavior of most of these people. They are aware that television has certain dangers within it and that the viewer, at least if he is as respectable as the accommodator thinks himself, needs to be cautious lest he be taken in unawares.

> I think TV is a wonderful medium of entertainment. I'd say it's quite important to us. I have only one thing against it, it's slightly hypnotic. The more you watch, the more you want to watch. I feel there are many things that slip by the way, intellectually speaking, though I still do a great deal of reading. But I'm sure that if we didn't have TV my husband would read more, and perhaps do more creative things around the house, not that he doesn't already do much more than most men do.

Thus, the accommodator is troubled from time to time by TV's enticing qualities, and he is tempted to qualify his acceptance. He claims not to watch as much as he actually does, he apologizes for his viewing behavior (and sometimes expresses downright guilt), and he says he prefers one type of program to another even though his behavior indicates the contrary. On occasion the ac-

commodator can sound almost like the protester, though
in most instances the difference is quite noticeable. He
may criticize an aspect of television, but he is not a critic
of the medium—and, more important, he does not see
himself in the latter role. He sees cause for caution but
not much reason for real protest. He may be keenly aware
of the controversial issues surrounding television—of
overindulgence, of wasted time and effort, of violence,
aggression, sex, and a host of "bad examples"—but he
does not feel that they should limit his enjoyment, though
they may lead him to write a judiciously complaining
letter.

One result of this ambivalence, however, is that the
accommodator watching television develops a considerable amount of self-consciousness. One such viewer says,
for example,

> I find that I watch it too much. I think I would do more
> things that I plan to do if I didn't watch television so much,
> like write letters and entertain more. Yet I find it relaxing. By
> 12:30 each day I'm pretty tired and find if I take a break it
> relaxes me. I can flop down on the sofa and watch Bob Cum-
> mings and really feel relaxed and ready to go on with my
> work.

The accommodator cannot use his set in the free-and-
easy, taken-for-granted, unplanned way that is characteristic of the "embracing" stance. An awareness of the
contending issues and an effort personally to do something about them create a deliberateness in how he
watches and makes use of TV. A sense of "struggling"
may be associated with this position, reflecting the pulls
and tugs the viewer feels exerted on him by his acceptance and enjoyment of TV and his reservations about it as
wasteful, enticing, and overly expressive of many undesirable feelings.

It is in terms of these attitudes that the accommodator seeks to balance the pros and cons of television and

to arrive at what he considers a judicious use of the medium. He may do this by compromising in how much time he and other members of his family spend watching his set, in deciding which programs are to be watched, or in thinking about what television ought ideally to be like —in all these instances attempting to strike a balance between what he feels to be the more extreme attitudes and behavior that other people may exhibit. For much the same reason, the accommodator is likely to be interested in and mindful of what the professional columnists and critics have to say, and, while he may not fashion his views in accord with theirs, he is inclined to take them into account. Above all, he will be sensitive to what is happening in television at any given moment—the changing styles of programs and personalities, the dominant criticisms, the most popular appeals, the standards of quality and taste that are widely acceptable, the loss of appeal and audience by a particular program and the rise of another—and he will modify his own views and tastes accordingly. He may not succeed in using television in quite the way he thinks would be ideal, but the degree of control he does achieve usually allows him to use it in very satisfying and enjoyable ways.

The Accommodators to Television

The accommodating group is not the largest of television's audiences, but it does appear to be one that is increasing in number and in importance. The process of accommodation makes inroads into the ranks of embracers and protesters as television becomes more commonplace and as viewers come to be more familiar and comfortable with it. As it loses some of its original luster and appeal, it becomes more readily integrated with other activities, interests, and satisfactions. This appears to have been happening for the past several years and is likely to continue for some years to come, altering in the process what television means and what it offers and how it is used and responded to by all viewers.

The Adult Lower Middle Class

At present the accommodating attitude is associated primarily with one main audience group, the mature, married, white-collar class of viewers. They range in age from the early twenties to the mid-fifties; they are in the process of forming a household, or they already have a family that is in the process of growing up. Occupationally, they are mainly in the white-collar group, with some skilled laborers and small-business owners among them. They are respectable, stable, conscientious, aspiring, goal-oriented, highly moral people. They value social participation, community responsibility, and education; their approach to most activities and objects is characterized by care, caution, and common sense. They are family- and home-centered individuals; child-rearing takes up much of their time and energy, and the issues of family, community, and morality are their dominant concerns. They comprise a growing number of people in present-day American society, whose attitudes and behavior have a pervasive influence in many areas of life, of which television is but one.

This audience can be divided into three subgroups—young married people, whose household is taking form; young parents, whose family is beginning to grow; and the stable family, in which the children range between mid-childhood and late adolescence. The attitudes and uses of television associated with each subgroup can be discussed separately.

Early married life is seen in two dominant ways: It is thought to be a relatively quiet and idyllic period, not yet involving the more responsible and time-consuming tasks of child-rearing. On the other hand, it is acknowledged to be an intense and involving time, a time for the spouses to set up a household, to get to know each other and establish (hopefully) a mutually satisfactory way of life. Early marriage implies the glitter, the glamour, the excitement of newness and fabled romance, as well as realistic discomfort with the unknown.

Young married persons, then, are absorbed with themselves and with beginning their mutual interrelations. Add to this the changing division of labor required when the wives work (and when typically both partners share in the care and maintenance of the home) and leisure time becomes more precious and more planned. There is no great need to seek leisure activities in the home; often there is a great deal of coming and going in this group—visiting, traveling, commercial entertainment. So, all in all, television usually is not a dominant focus of life, and young couples without children tend to be a highly selective audience.

Though the individual viewing patterns of the two spouses may be well entrenched, their viewing patterns as a couple are not as yet firmly established. This is a period of experimentation, in an effort to arrive at mutually acceptable and satisfying program choices. Television is not unique in this respect: the young couple is likely to be experimenting in many areas and with many different products in trying to arrive at agreement in their new way of life.

At this stage of life, our research shows, television is primarily thought of as an additional source of entertainment and stimulation. It is also thought to have educational value, in that it teaches about the world and serves as a guide for present and future family life. It serves a variety of additional functions as well, reflecting numerous motives:

> *It serves as a vehicle and test of mutual interests, as a focus of discussion, and as a method of arriving at mutual preferences (as to both programs and products).*

It is cheap, easy, and convenient, both as a form of enter-
tainment for the couple and as a way of relating to relatives
and friends.

It can help to reduce interpersonal tensions, which are com-
mon at this period of life, by providing absorbing material and
a focus of attention away from the spouse.

It provides established family models for learning methods
and values in family behavior and child-rearing.

It offers a variety of life-styles to choose from and aspire to
and can serve as a guide to current and established modes of
American life.

As for the content of entertainment, this group seeks a
high level of stimulation. They want programs that are
lively, absorbing, dramatic, and current. Those best liked
are often comedies, including the topical humor of those
comedians who embody cleverness as well as comic situations and stars whose humor derives in large measure
from an emphasis on changing values, fresh nuances, and
the very current meanings in our culture. Comedians of
the old style, like Jack Benny and Bob Hope, are prized
for their wit, timing, and acknowledged excellence.

Dramas and detective stories that depend on risqué
dialogue, romantic situations, irony, and challenge are
also liked. Discussion programs and panel shows that
provide quick repartee and innuendo are enjoyed for
their liveliness and underlying tone of unconventionality.
The imaginative Western, in the genre of *Gunsmoke* and
Maverick, is appealing, as are travel shows and adventure programs in exotic settings (*Hawaiian Eye, Adventures in Paradise,* etc.). Special and spectacular shows
that offer current themes and stars satisfy this group's
need for high stimulation, liveliness, and variety. As usual, men like a variety of sport programs, and a growing
number of young wives share this interest, or at least
make some effort to appear interested.

The shows that are disliked may include those that
strongly emphasize stereotyped and overly simplified
morality, as in the run-of-the-mill Western, the saccharine

family show, and some adventure stories. "Pretty music" of the Lawrence Welk type is thought to be boring, as is the variety format in general when it seems to offer the same people and the same format, the old songs and faded stars of the past.

Society considers the quiet idyll of early marriage to end as soon as a couple produces a child, for along with children come the problems of rearing them and a commitment to adult family life. Also, this is a stage when attempts to get established and settled are pronounced, when social horizons are greater, when parenthood is a quite self-conscious role, when children are more in the center of things, when one tends to expect more of himself. Life is full and very busy, and television is found to fit this situation in appropriate ways.

Television is often the chief means of entertainment of the growing family with young children. Because of the expense and, on the part of some young parents, an unwillingness to leave young children, most activities, including entertainment, are confined to the home. For adults, too, television is recognized as a good medium of entertainment, a continuing means of education in learning about the world, and a worthwhile addition to their lives. The worry that exists about passivity and the addictive pull of television is handled by more selective viewing and active control over how much time is spent watching and by keeping in touch with the issues in television criticism and the trends in TV tastes.

Viewing patterns for couples with growing children tend to be fairly regular, with some shows watched by the children and mother, some by the children and father, others by the family as a group. Still others are watched by the couple but not by the children, and by each partner alone. Because this group acknowledges a need for the diversion that TV offers, the main value of the medium is thought to stem from the entertainment and relaxation it provides. Less centrally and less explicitly, it also helps in mastering concern about parenthood and adult responsibilities. Primarily, its assets lie in the following realms:

> It serves to affirm family life and acts as a common focus for a total family unit.
> It provides guide posts for family affairs, things to do, ways to live, products to buy.
> It provides a retreat from the routine of everyday life and helps reduce family tension and anxiety by offering a world of adventure, excitement, and sensation.
> It permits the individual parent, as well as the couple as a family unit, to keep up with the world, to be informed about events and products, and, specifically, to know about what is going on in the television and entertainment world.
> It can provide isolation from family contacts, it can serve as a meeting ground between husband and wife, it can function as a way of entertaining relatives and friends, and it is a cheap and convenient baby sitter.

These people prefer programs that are current, stimulating, and varied in their moods and content. At this stage of life, there is particular appreciation of programs with a light touch, those that can be watched for sheer enjoyment. Family situations, if they are not too stylized, fall in this category; they often duplicate home and other familiar situations and allow for the release of many feelings in a humorous context. Parents like fast-paced variety, musical or otherwise, that presents an array of popular talent. The children are brought in to share these shows if there is confidence that they will be "decent" and "moral" so that parents can feel comfortable with the younger family members present.

Adult and family-type Westerns (*Wagon Train; Bonanza; Have Gun, Will Travel*) are interesting and stimulating to this audience segment. Among detective stories, they prefer those that are slick, sophisticated, intelligent, and well produced, such as *Hawaiian Eye* and *77 Sunset Strip*. A program like *The Untouchables* can make them feel a bit uncomfortable and troubled, though it is likely to be watched frequently, if not on a regular basis. Sports programs evoke a moderately high amount of interest, as do news broadcasts and special-event shows. In general, the educational format attracts attention, as do occasional dramatic shows that promise to be unusual. Quiz programs were liked by these viewers in our studies, particularly by the women, who also watch a few select daytime soap operas.

Programs that are too aggressive or otherwise overly forceful (some Western, adventure, and detective shows) are not accepted; and those that are experienced as too intellectual, subtle, or otherwise complex (some dramatic programs and discussion hours) are simply not enjoyed. But neither do these people like the "sweet and plain" shows, be they musicals or family-situation programs or dramas, unless they are "for the children."

The years between thirty-five and fifty are commonly defined as the "prime of life." They mark the peak of family solidarity and the beginnings of its disintegration. Parents of this age often have adolescent children who are on their way to increasing independence. The parental role changes and is diminished. Child-rearing no longer requires the constant vigilance of earlier days. Family members are free to pursue their separate and mutual lives, and husbands and wives are realigned to form again the basic unit.

This is a period of reflection, of thinking over what one has accomplished, and of re-establishing mutual and individual purposes and goals. There is sometimes a frantic desire to start anew, to accomplish something worthwhile before it is too late. For some, it is a period of enriched opportunities, a chance to pursue both old and new interests.

At this point, television presents more of a real choice as a form of entertainment and a pastime. Selectivity can be stronger, since more resources are available in and outside the home and since there is a feeling of greater freedom. During this life stage, the desire for intense stimulation tends to decrease, with a preference for less activity and, insofar as TV is concerned, for simpler, less demanding entertainment. On the whole, television continues to serve many of the same family functions as for younger couples before they have children, with some changes. Its main values lie in the following:

> It helps keep one younger and up-to-date, providing a broad range of life styles, ideologies, ideas, and knowledge. Sometimes it provides sufficient alternatives to encourage new interests.
>
> It gives one something to do and help pass the time, to some extent filling the void left by the growing-away of the children.

At this stage of life there is a gradual slipping into the "embraced" position that is commonly held by older people. This comes about with greater reliance on television and with less discriminating viewing habits; TV reasserts itself as a tried, true, and satisfying habit. Precisely when this shift occurs during the stable family years depends on many factors, but, in most instances, by the time people are in their mid-fifties the transition has been made. The undemanding, inexpensive, familiar, convenient meanings of television thus come to the fore and in the process may move the viewer from one audience group to another, each with its characteristic attitudes toward and patterns of using television.

In summary, the chapters in this first part have indicated how it is possible to generalize about relationships between audiences and programs, although each show requires individual study to analyze its specific appeal. Television's "embracers" are the least discriminating viewers and are apt to be found among children, old people, and lower-class people. The children are avid in their attention to television because it is an escape from the demands and pressures of the family environment and because it promises to illuminate the outside world of adults, of more expressive people, and of amazing events —whether these occur on news programs, Westerns, or commercials. Old people are avid in their attention to television also as an escape from their environment, but they wish still to feel part of life, and television promises them this. Working-class people combine both these general outlooks, finding in television a greater sense of participation in life than seems afforded them directly and an outlet for feelings less well socialized for them than for the middle class.

The occupation afforded by watching television often solves for embracers the problem of not knowing what to do. The easy absorption of television gives focus and expression to their inchoate or aimless feelings, and they are willing to settle for movement, liveliness, music, and any reasonably understandable working-out of relationships. As an audience, then, embracers are receptive to Westerns, situation comedy, variety shows, and soap opera. Here they find easy plot lines, bold outbursts, a sense of hilarity that makes them feel that they, too, understand and belong.

Television's "protesters" tend to set themselves in opposition to these values, to deride the idle pursuit of viewing pleasure. They want to substitute public purpose for self-indulgence, to emphasize reality rather than fantasy, to foster "culture" instead of "entertainment." They prefer news and public events programs and elevated drama, but there are divisions within the group. Some want high art; others want morality, to the point of excluding performers with notorious private lives or obnoxious examples of displeasing values.

The third group we have distinguished, the "accommodators," convey the most mixed and judicious attitudes. These are compounded of middle-class views and a busy absorption in daily life and accomplishment. This group believes that television fosters family-centered life, that it makes living easier, and that it affords some sophisticated stimulation when programs are well chosen. Their values are exemplified in sharp humor, plays with some maturity of dialogue or ambiguity of plot, clever Westerns, a general sense of currency, vitality, and variety. They are bored with stereotypes in Westerns, corny nostalgia, canned TV families, and too much intramural emphasis on show business as such. Television is to them mainly a resource, for both entertainment and education.

PART THREE

Television's Programs and Performers

The complexity of the television experience is great. The viewer, regardless of how he uses television and what feelings he has about it, finds that he is obligated continuously to confront a long, varied, and changing list of programs and entertainers. To select those that he might find satisfying, he must learn about them, evaluate them, and then decide which of various alternative offerings he will watch. The experience is made more complex by television's simultaneous presentation of competitive choices, since for most viewers there is more than one channel to watch, each with its own programs. A further complication is added by the fact that an individual viewer's selection of a particular program usually gets judged and arbitrated by others in his family with whom he shares a TV set. Their choices and preferences play a determining role in the programs and people he ultimately sees. On this basis, a complicated seeking-out and finding process continuously occurs among television's millions of viewers, with the result that in varying degree viewers find shows to their own satisfaction, and programs and performers succeed or fail in attracting large audiences.

The foregoing three chapters discussed some of the factors associated with different audience groups and what each of them hopes to derive from television. The following two chapters pertain to programs and performers, indicating how they come to attract, hold, or lose different viewers and audiences.

To the extent that television programs make their appeals in particular directions, they draw upon various categories of motivation. These categories form patterns, and on this basis it is possible to distinguish among different types of programs and performers—Westerns, drama, situation comedy, singers, cowboys, detectives, adventure heroes, etc. Thus, a type of program may take advantage of the appeals usually defined as masculine;

vigorous action normally orients a program toward men. However, a program type that combines action with concern for interpersonal relations is likely to raise feminine interest. If complexity of thought or elaboration of subjectivity is present, the program typically encourages people of higher social status to watch.

Out of the subtle patterning of such nuances and implications—expressed through the show's definition; its cast; its atmospheric tone; its symbolic content; the course and level of complication of its plot; its relative emphasis on ideas, movement, feelings, social or psychological ambiguities, etc.—come the characteristic meanings and appeals of a program type as well as the distinctions among specific shows within the type. These various factors accrue to create an image of the program type, and this image determines for whom the type is suitable, which audiences are likely to find pleasure in it and which ought not to watch it or will not want to watch it.

Program preferences vary with the social class, age, sex, family role, and personal needs of viewers, just as these factors relate to their general television attitude. The complex relationships between these variables and the main program types are not easily summarized. However, as a suggestive orientation to the discussion in Chapter 5, a simple scheme may help to show some over-all relationships among programs, sex, and social class, disregarding for the moment other aspects. The chart indicates generally which types of programs are more masculine or more feminine in appeal and which appeal to those of higher or lower social class.

Just as programs present clusters of symbols, each requiring a particular style of handling basic meanings and content, so, too, do performers present specialized modes of entertainment. Despite the fact that somewhere the performer leads a real life, what the audiences know are fictional derivations of these real lives, spiced with bits of information that may be true. Audiences develop sets of primary impressions in defining the television people they watch, and it is with these that they establish relationships. Entertainers become identified with a particular style, mode of expression, characteristic gesture or joke, with a certain program or role, or with other performers with whom they regularly appear. A musical variety star gets to be known by the way he sings a song, his manner of approach, his grooming, his mannerisms and habitual surroundings, and the set of background associates who appear with him. He may be thought of as loud, dramatic, winsome, affected, hostile, sexy, overly nice, strong, suspicious, or any possible clustering of real or imagined personal and symbolic traits. Types of performers become noted in terms of these identifications, values, and expectations, and within each type certain personalities can be seen as particularly good, average, or mediocre representatives.

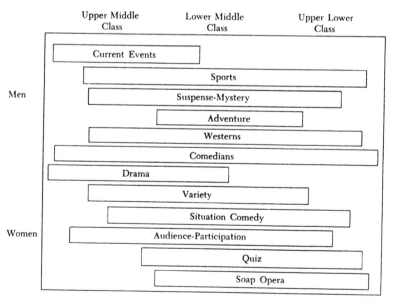

CHAPTER SIX

PROGRAM TYPES

Each of ten commonly watched program types is here discussed for its main meanings and attractions, and for the reactions it evokes from various audience groups. For many purposes, these ten types can be considered as the primary forms of TV entertainment. They do not readily change in appropriateness or appeal. What does change are the specific programs that most successfully represent each type at any particular moment of time and the relative balance among the ten different types.

It is evident in our surveys that people allow for—in fact, they often demand—different kinds of Westerns, comedy shows, situation comedies, quiz programs, etc. They are interested in new and different expressions of a basic program format. The success of any individual program will depend on how well it utilizes the meanings and appeals of the program type it represents, on the personalities it portrays, the stars it uses, the range and quality of feelings it evokes, and the competition it meets from other shows. It must also fit in with and measure up to the general taste patterns of the moment, a standard that is constantly shifting and forever vague but that always in some fashion reflects basic themes and values of the society and its individual members. The process of change is continuous, and it determines what types of programs will be made available and which will be most acceptable to viewers at any given time.

1. Westerns

Westerns occupy an especially favored place in American entertainment. They present a set of events, relationships, and meanings that have widespread appeal and that bear endless repetition. Many interpretations of the significance of the Western have been advanced, in terms that are historical, psychological, sociological, moral, and religious.

Westerns repeat aspects and elements of history, linking people with a past that is important in the development of our country. They reinforce a sense of a special kind of Americanism, a conception of pioneering frontiers that reverberates in the American outlook as a distinguishing characteristic and cause for pride. There is direct satisfaction in learning about homesteaders, Dodge City, the struggle between the sheep and cattle people, Red River, and all the heroes, villains, dance-hall queens, and schoolmarms who built the country.

Psychologically, in addition to these feelings of pride, marvel, and participation in the great past, Westerns arouse a vivid array of emotions. They have a persistent element of suspense as to how the ritual will be carried out in a particular instance. People can feel engaged without anxiety or guilt at the illusion of violence, even as they rock vicariously with the blows and shots.

Westerns work out family conflicts in a symbolic and projected fashion, and as in most theatrical experience, this is important in their appeal. In the Western, there appears a basic struggle for the reconciliation of a son with his antagonistic feelings toward his father and his wish to be a heroic man himself; he has mixed feelings toward his mother, in revering her purity but wondering how she can be a sexual object. These feelings are simplified by depicting father and mother as sharply good or evil, with the son triumphing over evil, whether it is external or in his own cowardice and weakness. The mother is symbolized in the heroine as sweet and virginal, and the dance-hall girl represents her lustier side in disguised form.

The moral nature of this struggle is often given as the basic justification for the Western. Guardians of the moral, conscientious aspects of our lives distinguish carefully among programs in describing their value: *Gunsmoke* is seen as offering "real moral teaching and less shooting and dying than most Westerns" and *Wyatt Earp* as "a show for the whole family and the whole nation to view with alarm." The most highly moralistic interpretation of the Western arises in those special instances in which the hero represents religious virtue in an extreme, distilled way. He is the mysterious stranger, appearing from nowhere, often enduring insult with overriding self-control, acting almost miraculously as savior of a beleaguered family.

The average viewer advances few such interpretations of Westerns. These dimensions of the entertainment are usually experienced as intrinsic, underlying one's awe, tension, avid repetitive interest, and willingness to see another minor variation on the durable themes.

> I like good Westerns with good story plots and actors. I have no definite reasons, I just like them.

When our respondents explained their enjoyment of Westerns, they usually described ideas of action, escape, the special attractions of performers, the general approach used in the show. A Western anthology series builds a feeling of continuity, a familiarity with the characters that can heighten the viewer's involvement and participation.

> *Gunsmoke* I like. I like Marshall Dillon, Kitty and Chester. I like the stories they have, that type. They have the same principals playing in there week after week so that you feel you know them. They don't change them around.

Gunsmoke . . . I like all of this cast. They seem like real people.

In recent years *Gunsmoke* has presented the Western in a particularly endearing way, leading people to call it predictable, believable, realistic, and "homey." The cast has formed a stable, familial set of relationships that rescues it from too much simplicity or starkness. *Wagon Train* is a similarly excellent blending of familiar and novel elements, relatively mature issues, and the personal appeal of the late Ward Bond and Robert Horton.

Westerns appeal primarily to youthful and masculine interests. That is, they are supposed to find their main audience among men and children. While women generally blame males or yield to them as the ones seeking the rough outdoors, fighting, and horses, many women also become part of a large and appreciative audience. Half of a Western's regular audience may be women, although in one sample we studied only 13 per cent of the regular women watchers expressed an active preference for the particular show.

> We see Bat Masterson regularly. . . . My husband will watch Johnny Ringo if I'm not here. He's a real cowboy fan. If I can flip the switch right quick, we'll see Pat Boone. If he catches me, we'll have to see *Zane Gray Theatre*.

> At night it's Westerns. My husband likes cowboys and I watch with him. At night my husband decides what we will see. I like comedies.

A women's interest in a Western tends to increase when women play a larger role, when romance or family is involved.

The many appeals of Westerns are by no means class-bound; upper-middle-class people are often as interested in them as are lower-class people. However, since the former watch less television on the average and are generally more selective, they are likely to fix on fewer favorites and to emphasize those with greater individuality. Westerns often produce mixed feelings in upper-middle-class people, since they regard them as mass entertainment with a normally low level of quality, especially when such programs proliferate as they have on TV. Also, these people feel that their violence is excessive, even in a moral cause, or that there is undue glorification of a questionable era of conquest and unruliness. At the same time, they can find undeniable enjoyment in Westerns. These mixed attitudes were expressed by one upper-middle-class man when looking at a television program booklet.

> Looks to me like they're all cowboys. Why don't they get away from those damn cowboy pictures? From six o'clock to ten they've got 1-2-3-4-5-6-7 cowboy pictures, isn't that terrible! .... You want to know something? I hate to tell you this, but if I watched TV more than I do, I'd probably look for these Western programs.

2. Comedy

Comedy is a very broad television category. It encompasses at least three main types of shows: situation comedies, comedians, and cartoons. In addition, humor and comic action are enjoyed during the adventures of a "private eye" or a Western hero as well.

Humor is a fundamental and human way of dealing with life. It is a technique for achieving some discharge of deep-seated impulses (particularly aggressive impulses) while simultaneously taking the edge off them or seeming to deny their force. Comedy seems to skim the surface of life, to deal with events as though they were not of real significance or consequence. At the same time, the best comedy shows its merit by diving deeply at times, giving a sense of revelation.

In explaining their enjoyment of comedy, people note either the distraction or the insight provided. They are taken away from their own difficulties or feel more reconciled to them.

> I like to laugh . . . *December Bride* is a funny show. They get into a lot of trouble. Spring Byington is the star.

> *Father Knows Best* and *Danny Thomas* are comedies that I enjoy because they get your mind off of everyday problems.

Many situation comedies are favored both in their first showings and in reruns. Many references are made to Lucille Ball's shows, to *My Little Margie, Gale Storm, December Bride, The Real McCoys, Ozzie and Harriet, Dobie Gillis, Dennis the Menace, Leave It to Beaver, Topper,* Ann Sothern, Donna Reed, etc. These are relatively undemanding shows; they come and go, leaving a moment of brightness and hilarity, and now and then a touch of warmth. They are part of the mental hygiene of everyday life.

> If I watch comedies in the daytime, I seem to be in a better humor at night. I love what I see on TV. I'm stimulated by it.

Probably the outstanding situation comedy in recent years has been *Father Knows Best.* Its popularity is general and great; it combines elements of variety, realism, and surprise, giving a vivid sense of how ordinary people can solve problems. It functions to make life seem manageable and agreeable. It reminds everyone that they all share the customary problems of child-rearing, family life, and neighborhood social relations. In talking about this show, people do not particularly emphasize the cast, since the comedy family has become an integral part of the show and the performers are taken for granted.

> *Father Knows Best,* that one is tops. The children and I always watch it. Excellent actors. And the story—good morals for the children, and human situations. I think that one promotes better family relations. *The Danny Thomas Show* is cute too, but not always.

Father Knows Best is the kind of show that almost everyone has seen on television at one time or another, and in general the category of comedy is of wide interest. These shows are for everyone, but perhaps a bit less for men than for women. They do not exclude men, in the sense that Westerns to some degree "exclude" women, but it is recognized that comedy shows are likely to emphasize feminine values to some degree in their familial orientation. The audience can be broad because comedy shows tend to be nonviolent, simple in plot, readily grasped by youthful minds, perhaps noisy and active, but mild in emotional tone. Women especially like them because their wholesomeness and broad appeal reinforce their family aims; men can also approve.

> They are family programs and my family is my interest.
>
> *Donna Reed Show* . . . seems to be a family show. My daughter gets a kick out of how the mother and father get children out of situations that are ticklish children's tricks, you know, and things that they do. I like that myself. More or less the fact that they realize how they've been helped out of their troubles. There's a moral to them; like Aesop's fables, they tell a story and tell a moral at the end. A modern setting of the old format, and a very good idea.

Comedies are thought to appeal less to people whose interests most sharply move away from solid, middle-class, familial kinds of absorption in television. Those less interested include teen-agers, single young adults, and men of both high and low social status.

The appeal of comedians is that of the comedy form generally, but their individual style determines their particular audience. Most people take definite stands on comedians, having distinct favorites and pet peeves. Some specific entertainers are discussed in the following chapter, on TV personalities.

3. Variety

Walter Kerr[*] has expressed the thesis that television is at its intrinsic best when it presents a visual essay on a topic that could hardly be handled in the same way by

[*]"What Good Is Television," *Horizon*, II (March, 1960), 4.

any other medium. Others believe that TV is uniquely
effective with on-the-spot news of special significance, and
a third view is that TV is destined to be an unsurpassed
avenue for education. But there remains the widespread
notion that TV has yet to realize its latent potentialities.

In practice, however, and as most people actually experience television and seek to experience it, the variety
show probably comes closest to fulfilling TV's destiny.
This may not be socially desirable, looking toward the
potential values of the medium, especially as these are
desired by the "protesting" viewers. Nevertheless, the variety show is especially gratifying to many people, since
it satisfies their central motives for viewing TV. These
shows are suited to the definition of television as something to be used in transient ways. They most specifically
express the entertainment nature of the medium. They offer the utmost in relaxation, insofar as this implies little
muscular, intellectual, or emotional tension on the part
of the viewer. They permit a low level of commitment
by people who are wary of seeming intensely attached
and a blandness of participation by people who are not
seeking intense or emotionally demanding experiences.

A basic dynamic process in a preference for variety
shows is the relief of boredom. Feelings of boredom occur when people are uncertain about what they want to
do, when they have unconscious yearnings toward un-
identified impulses and objects. Their attention is then
like a scanning device that is resistant to close focusing
on a sustained set of ideas, and they hope distractedly
to grasp a tidbit of gratification from what passes before
them. Variety shows are safe outlets for moral, middle-
class people, allowing them a modest degree of titillation of their impulses.

Perhaps most distinctively, variety shows capture the
quality of glamour in show business and make it casu-

ally available in the home—and this is one of the most marvelous and enduringly attractive things about television. In any given instance, a variety show might not be preferred to some other type of program, and any given variety show may rise and fall in public favor. But people have an insatiable urge to watch the exhibition of specific talents, to see personalities either performing their special roles or merely appearing in order that the audience may get a good look at them. Not only is it esthetically interesting and entertaining to watch a skilled person perform; variety shows also feed fantasies of fame and fortune. They provide a chance for a closer knowledge of the entertainer and contribute to feelings of indulgence and opulence at the feast being presented in the home.

Variety shows are usually associated with a major star, who is the central entertainer and/or master of ceremonies (such as Perry Como, Ed Sullivan, Dinah Shore, and Garry Moore), or who may be chosen to present a special or spectacular show (such as Fred Astaire or Frank Sinatra). A good variety show is one with sufficient variety, though it may be linked in a meaningful way to an organizing idea or person to lend it some sense of rationale —even if this be only as tenuous as Ed Sullivan's presentation of vaudeville acts. These shows are expected to be musical, lively, and good humored, not too labored, to have "good guest stars," and, hopefully, some measure of unexpected occurrence—an unusual performance, a distinctive feat, a successful stepping-out of character, a new find, a momentary seriousness or bit of sentiment.

Ed Sullivan would be the program I like the best because of the variety. I enjoy it when there is good music or dancing.

Now the *Perry Como Show* at 8 P.M. is good. We watch him about twice a month. Ordinarily I try to settle the children and their homework upstairs before that. My husband also likes Perry Como, his personality and good selection of guests.

Variety shows are regarded as suitable entertainment for everyone, agreeable for the whole family. This is because they are usually presented in the evening, at the most convenient hours, and are thought to be bland enough for children and offensive to no one. Like comedy (which is often included in them), their blandness, their relative emphasis on personal expressiveness, display, and generalized enjoyment, tends to shift their appeal away from men. Over all, women and younger people are the most responsive audience, although men are not thought to be excluded. Despite the youthful appeal of variety shows, older people usually constitute an important part of their audience.

As with comedy, variety shows appeal to people of both middle- and lower-class levels. However, comedies tend to carry stricter social-class definitions, being generally a bit more "lower class" in implication, with middle-class interest selecting "worthier" forms of humor. Variety has a relatively stronger appeal to the middle-class group, since it seems more individual, more skillfully controlled, and more sophisticated. It is also more acceptable as a means of relaxing and using television without being too much beguiled by it.

4. Suspense and Mystery

In comparision with comedy and variety, the suspense-mystery category taps much more intense motives. It involves higher levels of excitement, curiosity, and intellectual challenge. As do Westerns, these shows pose issues of good and evil, the ultimate triumph of justice, law, and order, but their contemporaneity can make them extremely vivid in their treatment of such problems. Often the success of the protagonist in these shows bypasses conventional channels of authority. This permits the viewer to identify more directly with the idea that he might be engaged in astute behavior and heroic events outside the conventionally defined role of constituted authority.

The range of suspense-mystery qualities is broad. Suspense may be the predominant factor, appealing to the active arousal of emotions of foreboding and anticipation. Here anxiety about something that might take one unawares and a wish for resolution are likely to be strong, and these feelings are relieved by action and by finding out the answer. In other instances, the puzzle predominates, to be solved by clues, logic, and insight. Here the viewer's satisfaction is more intellectual, with wonderment and curiosity relieved by cleverness.

Extreme suspense tends to rest in a fascination with some drastic action that seems inevitable. The viewer feels transfixed with ambivalence, unable to believe that the terror can be averted, hoping against hope that it can. The deeper, personal analogue is a wish to be overwhelmed by some dark inner or outer force and to survive the awful knowledge that comes with it.

At the heart of all suspense and mystery programs is the quest for revelation. The audience is trying to figure out what can happen in life when deep, basic forces in the human personality are unleashed. Ignoring the problems of daily life that need to be solved to maintain the family, the suspense-mystery shows moves into the outside world and the underworld of emotions and actions where interpersonal relations are passionate, secretive, greedy, and threatening to broad social norms. These shows work out a compromise between negative impulses and rebellion against the demands of other people (with the core motives of destroying and taking) and the need to live with other people (and, therefore, to take revenge and make restitution). Suspense-mystery stories reassure people that *they* did not do it, even though they felt like doing it. Possibly at the heart of the matter is the childish wish to find out what goes on behind adults' closed doors, sustaining the classical appeal of the locked-room mysteries. These shows are provocative and sometimes controversial because they often combine violence and eroticism or hint at sophisticated or perverse relationships.

A relatively pure form of the mystery category is the *Perry Mason Show*. Here a legal struggle is joined with a puzzle, to dramatize strikingly the major issues of bafflement and social restoration, distilled and brought to a focus in the courtroom.

> We don't watch anything on Saturday until 6:30, when we watch *Perry Mason*. I like it very much because it is a courtroom drama. I think the actors are very convincing in their roles, especially Raymond Burr.

The characters and format of *77 Sunset Strip* have given this series a wide appeal, especially among younger viewers.

> At 8 P.M. it's *77 Sunset Strip*. It's not tripe. It's the children's choice—a little jazzy, but I watch it with them.

> I don't look at any of the programs until *77 Sunset Strip* comes on and I really like that. It's always a good mystery story and I can relax and enjoy it.

Suspense and mystery shows are regarded as moderate in their appeal to women and older people. Their major audience is among men and young people. Women whom we interviewed discussed much of their watching without ever mentioning a suspense or mystery show. Mature women are generally apt to find them too intense and too threatening to seem appealing, even though this group also contributes avid watchers. Sometimes they lump them negatively with Westerns as providing an excess of crime and violence on TV. These shows are on the men's side of the audience-show spectrum, since they are not specifically oriented to supporting and maintaining the familial status quo and do not lend support to constructive feminity.

> At 9 P.M. the kids go to bed. Then my husband picks the programs. At 9 we watch *M-Squad* on Channel 5. It's

about the police department. It's lousy. Nine-thirty he likes *Grand Jury* on Channel 5. It's about the police and fighting crime. I hate it.

Not only are men the focal audience for suspense-mystery plays, but men of higher status find this kind of entertainment most appealing. Specific programs have wide attraction across social-class lines—including *Perry Mason, 77 Sunset Strip, Hawaiian Eye, The Untouchables,* —but a persistent interest in such shows as *Bourbon Street Beat, Peter Gunn, Markham, Philip Marlowe,* or *The Thin Man* draws from a middle-class masculine audience to a great extent. People of higher status are responsive to the aggressive, intellectual, and sophisticated elements in these stories and to their implications of effective social control that can be exercised by poised, adept, civilized, and clever men.

5. Drama

Drama is a broad category and might, in fact, include Westerns, suspense-mystery shows, or any theatrical performance in play form. Here it is taken to refer to programs that offer "plays" rather than repetitive content; the form dominates rather than the domain of content emphasized. In this sense, for example, it is not clear whether *Alfred Hitchcock Presents* is a series of dramas or a suspense-mystery series. People talk of it as the latter, but there is probably sufficient variety of content and emphasis on interpersonal and psychological material to call it a dramatic series.

Since plays can be about almost anything, their meanings are infinite. As a television category, their significance and the motives for enjoying them are more specific. It is ordinarily assumed that drama will have—or seek to attain—some special merit in involving its audience. It is ideally expected to do so not through mere excitement or sensationalism but rather through the manipulation of elements that are peculiarly theatrical, somehow related to the legitimate stage, with special communications deriving from the plot and the skill of the cast as actors rather than personalities, however important the stars may be.

Drama is an aspiring human endeavor, then, a large attempt to understand and make comprehensible the nature of human life in ways that are important. Dramas are supposed to be introspective, cultured, cultural, and esthetic. These values are essentially snobbish and are most proudly held by upper-middle-class and mobile elite-minded groups, but they are concurred in by lower-status people also. Thus, drama is regarded as "high-class" entertainment, to be admired and respected as well as, hopefully, enjoyed. Violence and sexual content are more permissible in this form, where they are defined as illuminations of the human soul and its frailties rather than as the titillation of base impulses as presented in crime shows or by sexy guest stars.

The dramatic category is very demanding of attention. It involves something meaty, often somber, fraught with subtle as well as obvious meanings. It goes on at a relatively high pitch of emotional and intellectual stimulation. The audience is expected to get involved, to work at understanding, and to read things into it and get things out of it. They ordinarily expect to be impressed, particularly by the performance. The most commonly expressed reasons for admiring plays revolve around the excellence of the point made by the drama and the excellence of the acting.

Ingrid Bergman in "Turn of the Screw"—magnificent!

There is one show I plan to watch tomorrow night. It's a special one. Helen Hayes is in it, and I just think she is one of the most wonderful people on the stage . . . . Any time she is in anything, I try to see it because she is such a marvelous actress.

Drama in TV is represented by certain regular series and some intermittent special programs. Among the outstanding dramatic offerings of highest status is *Playhouse 90*, which is the "grand old drama" of television. While it (and other admired shows) rarely come up in spontaneous discussions of television watching, it is prominently to the fore when middle-class people want to indicate that their television habits and preferences are of a high order. Similar in status are such offerings as *United States Steel Hour* and *Hallmark Hall of Fame*.

Alfred Hitchcock and Loretta Young are the two outstanding producers of play series. Both have general appeal, Hitchcock being of higher status and sophistication and having a more masculine orientation.

> I like a good mystery and he has a good mystery show.

> The wife and I watch Hitchcock; we don't like it for our son (8 years old) to see this 'cause he doesn't understand them. They are a little too deep for him yet.

The *Loretta Young Show* is much admired, especially by working-class and white-collar women who appreciate Miss Young's clothes and the moral qualities of her productions.

> Well, Loretta Young plays in her shows. Most of her plays have some sort of moral lesson in them. I enjoy watching her act a great deal. It's interesting because she portrays so many characters.

The audience for drama is practically universal, in that most people can respond to and be absorbed by a play. As a genre, however, drama appeals most centrally to adult middle-class people, especially of the higher status levels, and to women. Plays are more directly concerned with human issues, emotions, and reactions than are other forms of television entertainment, making women feel they are in their proper province as keepers of the emotions. But plays cannot be defined so narrowly, and their content varies so much that men are not at all excluded from interest in them. In general, the people who respond to plays, seek them out, and watch them in preference to other things are likely to feel mature and part of an elite, superior to those who prefer run-of-the-mill fare and the less stimulating types of entertainment.

6. Quiz and Audience Participation Shows

Shows in this category usually involve an emphasis on real people rather than on fantasy characters or on professional performers in their formal roles. The participants are supposed to be behaving as amateurs or representatives from private life, whether in fact this is true or not. Their rewards for appearing are payments that are supposed to be public matters and judged by standards other than regular professional scales. Thus, people win prizes, objects, and sums in keeping with their achievement on the program, or sometimes they are known to get a token payment merely for being a guest.

This special nature governs the basic relationship of the audience to such programs. It rests in the supposedly realistic exposure of personalities and consequently permits a kind of face-to-face implication that can transcend ordinary entertainment. It is this definition that explains the public shock of the quiz show exposés, which showed that "friends" were deceitful. At heart, many people recognize the show-business nature of even these programs and heartily wish they were back, even if the contestants are paid or do put on a "rigged" performance. The reality of quiz and participation shows does not really have to be real.

The realistic element is nonetheless important and operates in different ways. Three main program groupings may be noted. One is the typical quiz or prize show, such as *The Price Is Right* or *Concentration*. Here the audience is motivated by rooting for particular people to win and by their own vicarious or envious dreams. At the core of their thoughts is "that could be me, I wish it were." They enjoy testing their own knowledge. In addition, the master of ceremonies is usually seen as a man with an attractive personality, a cross between a benevolent, giving father and a very cheerful son. The audience often becomes fond of these men, taking their television personalities for fact.

> Well, the one that I like is *The Price Is Right.* I love to see people win things . . . . I enjoy *Queen for a Day* with Jack Bailey . . . . Occasionally I watch *Beat the Clock* because they have some nice prizes on there too for the contestants to win.

> Bill Cullen is the M.C. on *The Price Is Right.* Well, they give away a lot of gifts on that quiz show. I would like to have them myself.

These shows have a particularly distinctive appeal to working-class housewives, who can in this way look in on other people's lives in a context that implies real (if glamorous and miraculous) problem-solving. The shows imply a world of mature women who can relax and be giggling girls again under the stimulating good humor of the master of ceremonies. The viewers can revel in a feeling of material relief and gratification, and this appeal is not limited to older women, although they may predominate in the audience. An eighteen-year-old girl comments:

> My mother watches *Concentration* every day . . . . She watches *It Could Be You* at 11:30. Bill Leyden M.C.'s it. I sometimes watch it myself. I like to see the looks on the people's faces when they're surprised.

A second group within this category includes the quiz, prize, or contest show that relies on celebrities and show-business personnel. This reduces the sense of direct identification felt by the audience and the emphasis on material rewards, but a sense of good humor is elevated at the constant joke seen in the incongruity of performers doing something unprofessional or pretending to be ordinary people. Also, the glamorous aspects of "star-gazing" provide pleasure, as in *The Arthur Murray Party, Masquerade Party,* and *I've Got a Secret.* Sometimes these programs are more like variety shows than quiz shows, as is suggested by people who say:

> We always watch *Ford Startime, Arthur Murray Party,* and *Garry Moore* sometimes. They're all variety shows.

These shows have a strong atmosphere of cheerful, hectic entertainment, not highly organized despite a set format. Their appeal is broader and more general than the first category of quiz shows. Middle-class and some younger people are apt to be interested, although women are still likely to predominate.

> Occasionally I watch *The Arthur Murray Show.* They have good music. I enjoy good music. They have celebrities, people that I didn't know could dance. It's interesting to see who will be on.

Men find such shows relatively lacking in purpose—they want their looking-in to be less like mere peeping at the stars.

> *The Rifleman* has a wonderful example for children. In every story it is based on a small child and a good example. Programs like *Arthur Murray, Dobie Gillis,* and *Keep Talking* are asinine.

The third group in this general category includes the more sophisticated conversation shows. Here there remains an element of looking in on celebrities as their real selves or as different from their customary roles. The casualness of unexpected interactions and remarks carries the implication that spontaneous revelations will occur. Viewers are constantly on the alert for surprising insights into the "real" nature of the stars. This preoccupation is satirized in frequent references to "what is Jack Paar *really* like?" Normally, some intellectual elements are present.

Outstanding examples in this group are *"The Jack Paar Show, Person-to-Person,* Susskind's *Open End* and Kupcinet's *At Random." What's My Line?* probably stands between this and the foregoing type. With these shows, much depends on who appears, and this makes audience interest somewhat variable.

> Sometimes we watch Jack Paar, but it depends on his guest stars, and his personality that night .... *Person-to-Person* we aim for, my husband and I, sometimes the children too, if it's not too crazy, as they say, but it depends on the subject.

> *The Jack Paar Show* I like for the reason he usually has interesting personalities. It is one program where the public can see top celebrities out of the roles they play in their television and stage careers.

These shows encompass a wide range in the status of their audiences, but they are generally more acceptable to people of higher status than are the previously mentioned two groups. A feminine emphasis is still present, but not as exclusively, since men find some attraction in debates and in the airing of views, sometimes in wit and in the range of people involved. Since this range usually is broad and varied, the appeal of such programs is enlarged.

7. Adventure

Adventure shows usually occur in an exotic locale, removed in time or geography. They ordinarily involve strong action and frequently some struggle with the forces of nature or with foreign, hostile elements. They are distinguished from Westerns, mysteries, and dramas (which may all be variations of adventure shows) by their relatively lighter emphasis on the human aspects of interpersonal relationships. Often there is an interest in exploration and discovery, a specific and strange environment (ice, forest, water), or in events that are novel, large-scale, or amazing. A grand sense of triumph may be sought that is bigger or more awe-inspiring than the gratifyingly successful resolution of less adventurous activities. The effort is great; the reward is in keeping. Often, of course, these elements are not present in notable degree, the adventure plot presenting the same conflicts as do the typical Western.

Adventures, because of their locations and because they seem often to imply some larger kind of personal or social motivation, may have an educational tinge and can be justified as instructive in some way. Of this latter sort, Lowell Thomas and John Gunther represent fairly extreme and outstanding versions.

> If we haven't turned on *Perry Mason* for some reason, then at 7:00 we turn on *High Road* .... You see how people get along in different parts of the world, what they do, how they live.

> Well, I like to watch *High Road*. John Gunther has some very good programs; he takes you away from home to places far away.

The fundamental aim of getting away from one's own environment to fantasies of other places, with their novelty and excitement, is also highlighted in such shows as *Sea Hunt* and *Adventures in Paradise*.

> At 8:30 on Monday there's also *Adventures in Paradise*. My husband likes it very much—good guest stars—never trite—and a *perfect* escape!

The appeal of adventures is broad. They offend no particular group and seem worthwhile for children without being too immature for adults. Insofar as they are basically action shows and stress mastery of the physical environment, they tend to appeal relatively more to men than to women. In such settings women are usually diminished or degraded and the power of men is glorified; women are more likely to be attracted in proportion to the amount of emphasis placed on human interest and the presence of a love interest. Documentary qualities increase watching at the upper-middle-class level; otherwise, the adventure show is a middle-class show, attracting those of moderate status.

8. Education

Educational programs are widely regarded as TV at its finest, whether such shows are watched or not. Most obviously, they appeal to the viewer's wish to learn, to know, to enlarge himself by factual information and understanding the world around him. To some, education is defined in the formal terms of the classroom, via qualified authority, didactic procedures, and some removal from the practical concerns of daily life to a more theoretical level. At its extreme, this orientation manifests itself in "educational television" on especially reserved channels. Vaguely, education is thought also to be some part of the obligation of licensed commercial channels.

A great part of this attitude consists of a façade of virtue; people give lip service to learning and its superiority, while seeking excitement and the gratification of less admired and easier goals. Education that is presented in a genuinely exciting way is attractive to most people, of course. They prefer to learn without realizing they are doing so, where there are no drills or authorities to compel them and where there is a human dramatization of the process. They do not see why education has to seem—as do so many programs on the educational channels—drab, gray, inept, dull, prissy, passive, self-righteous, noncommunicative, or impractical.

> I think one place that TV falls down is with informative programs. There should be educational forums or programs on it—and if they present it in an entertaining way, they'd be doing a good job.

For these reasons, the programs that people admire for their educational values are those that best mask or combine their didactic aspects with theatrical elements.

These may draw upon the vaudevillian (*Captain Kangaroo*), the drama of the movies in montage and documentation (*Twentieth Century*), the prestige and authoritative talent of the theater or concert hall (Leonard Bernstein, Agnes DeMille), and an easy immersion in science and "culture" (*Bell Telephone Hour*).

There is a general notion that educational programs ought to appeal to everyone, that they are "good" for everyone, and sometimes this feeling is acted upon:

> First we watch *Popeye*, then we watch *Twentieth Century* because of the historical background. It is one of the educational things we enjoy together.

While nearly everyone expresses a virtuous interest in educational programs, many see them as directed primarily toward old people and children, because the former no longer have vital interests and the latter are still learning. One result is that educational programs tend to be squeezed out of the watching schedule by program types with higher priorities on most people's interest. Such programs are likely to find their real audiences among smaller groups who give more than lip service to their educational outlook. These are people with intellectual or intellectualized points of view: rather serious middle-class men, women who want to keep up with their husbands' broader perspectives, parents who are solicitous about their children's education, upper-middle-class people, and, most generally, those who view TV from the protester's perspective.

9. News and Current Events

News and current events are casually included as a normal and essential part of television fare. The motivation for watching them is taken for granted, as a serious, reasonable curiosity about what goes on in the world. The audience feels it is keeping up appropriately by giving attention to such programs.

> I watch the news to increase my knowledge of world affairs
> that I wouldn't get otherwise. It gives me something to dis-
> cuss with friends and other people.

The basic motives for this interest are the same as those
that support reading the newspapers. Television, much
like radio, gives, in addition, rapid summaries of events
regarded as significant, information that can readily be
absorbed while people are doing other things, such as
shaving, eating breakfast, having dinner, etc. TV provides
a view of the speaker if desired and a presentation that
gives the event greater vividness and immediacy than can
the spoken word alone. Weather information on TV has
probably raised meteorological understanding to a new
high. The ability of television to bring an important on-
going event into the home is one of its most dramatic attributes, and this is highlighted by the coverage of such
events as political conventions, Khrushchev's visit, the
Olympic games, the World Series, the "Great Debates"
between presidential candidates, etc.

Newscasts and commentaries tend to be seen in terms
of the people who present them. Some have particular
reputations and develop loyal audiences, who prefer
their methods of presentation. Huntley and Brinkley,
John Daly, Douglas Edwards, Frank Blair, and local people, too, stand out in viewers' minds.

Most viewers have some awareness of news programs
and may pick up something from the morning, late afternoon and evening shows. Still, the average viewer is able
to talk at length about television without mentioning
these programs. The people who are more likely to focus
on this area are those who otherwise pay little attention
to world news, and especially men, who feel it is part of
their responsible manliness to be knowing about significant events. Upper-middle-class people admire television
particularly for its potentialities in bringing the outside
world to the mass of people. They see this as one of its
primary legitimating features.

I think it has a definite educational value, particularly from a news standpoint. It is faster for me to watch Garroway than read the newspaper because I'm a lousy newspaper reader. It is easier; there's very little effort. And the sports events, like the Olympics, that was tremendous! And educational and beneficial to the family as a unit. But the Westerns and the love stories and particularly the whores from Hollywood, I think that's the big drag and is detrimental to family life.

They are certain to progress, that's only natural. I expect more events as they are happening, more than you get now. Like the President's trip, you get films a day or two after the thing has happened. I expect you will get more on-the-spot happenings; in other words, you will see them as they are taking place.

Thus, news and current events have the generally virtuous atmosphere of educational programs and are "good" for everybody. Similarly their specific appeal is upgraded in status, often ignored in reality, and attended to by the more mature and responsible people in the audience. Sporting events are exceptional, acting as a great leveler by their broad appeal to the young and the mature, to men of all social classes, and to many women as well.

10. Soap Opera

The appeals of soap operas are basically the same on television as they were on radio. These were studied by Warner and Henry, who, in their monograph, *The Radio Daytime Serial*, summed up their meaning and significance in this way:

The primary social function of the program is to strengthen and stabilize the basic social structure of our society, the family. It so functions by dramatizing family crises and the ideals and values involved, as they are understood and felt by the women who listen and by making the good wife the center of action and power.*

The soap opera provides the viewer with an on-going

*W. Lloyd Warner and William E. Henry, *The Radio Daytime Serial: A Symbolic Analysis*, "Genetic Psychology Monographs" (1948), No. 37, p. 64.

relationship with a group of familiar characters, building a sense of intimacy, of looking in on the lives of other people struggling to get along. This reassures the viewer either that life can be worse than one's own is or that the many problems that occur can be mastered or survived. Sometimes this material is meaningful to a viewer to a degree that cannot be tolerated.

> *Love of Life* must be a serial. I don't care for them . . . . I don't watch any soap operas. They're too sad. I feel too tense when I watch them.

Soap operas are one of the most clearly and sharply defined types of program on TV. They are essentially the woman's private domain, with men rejecting them as daytime shows for women, though they may sometimes watch on a companionable basis. This may lead them to get caught up in the story line and to find soap operas more appealing than their general definition suggests. One such man says:

> In the later afternoon I see *The Edge of Night* . . . . When I watch those late afternoon shows it's usually because my wife has the TV on and I come in about that time, so I sit down and watch 'em with her . . . . I haven't seen any during the afternoon except maybe *The Edge of Night* and *The Brighter Day* and *The Secret Storm* . . . . Those continued things do pretty well, sort of like reading a story that goes on and on.

Relatively mature, middle-class women find soap operas absorbing—sometimes only casually justified, but still an important way of seeing life.

> *Love of Life* is a serial, it's a life story, a story of real life. There's no special reason I look at it, it's just the time that I like to sit and have a cup of coffee and watch TV. It's a real life story based on real life.

> Most of the afternoon watchings are what we call soap operas and they're very good . . . . I like to see them. They present home life. Real life happenings . . . . the ups and downs that most every family has. I like to see somebody I think has a harder time than I do.

Upper-middle-class women are much less likely to find enjoyment or absorption in soap operas. Although they are not totally absent from the audience, their typical attitude is to dismiss the genre as beneath notice, as an exaggerated, monotonous view of life. The soap opera chooses so sharply among feminine audiences because it emphasizes a particular view of family relations. In its barest form, it says that the woman is the dominant figure in the home, that she must be strong in dealing with illness, predatory women, weak husbands, etc.—all the forces that may threaten the integrity of the family unit. Such ideas are consequently most appealing to working-class women, who feel most beset and least able to cope with disaster or disruption.

From the foregoing analyses, some general conclusions may be drawn. The standards that people bring to bear in judging television shows vary with the type of show and the personalities involved, the audience group, other available programs, and similar considerations. In judging a performance or a performer, a wide range of variables will be employed as the bases for approval or disapproval, enjoyment or displeasure. In a brief series of comments a single viewer called upon such attributes as naturalness, restraint, virtue, talent, versatility, cleverness, understanding, currency, piety, vastness, egotism, repetition, consistency, and immaturity. Similarly, any given show represents its program type in particular ways and puts forth the pertinent variables in an individual manner.

As has been shown, motivational elements that are tapped by television shows include:

> *Historical and national pride:* This is involved in Westerns, in special current events programs, in people who exemplify the democratic ethos.
>
> *Basic familial struggles:* These are symbolically or di-

rectly presented by most television shows in one way or another, most importantly in Westerns, mysteries, comedies, dramas, and soap operas. The focus and style vary. Westerns are a classic ritualization of the Oedipus situation, in which the son contends with authority and seeks his mother's love. Sibling hatreds can find expression in the conflict of gangsters and detectives. *Dennis the Menace* presents a particular flouting of adult regulation, and Dobie Gillis' father finds his son's irresponsible concern with adolescent sexuality especially trying. How the various familial issues are handled gives a program its special character, through its subtlety, superficiality, intensity, dominant figures, candor, etc.

Masculine pride: Shows vary in their evaluation of manly aims and status. Westerns, mysteries, adventures, and sports flatter the prowess of men in conquering opposing forces through their moral, intellectual, and physical superiority.

Feminine pride: Perhaps fewer shows are aimed at flattering women and their roles than at men. Soap operas qualify, as do some dramas, comedies, variety shows, and the outstanding women, such as Dinah Shore, Loretta Young, Jane Wyman, and Lucille Ball.

Curiosity: This is an intense motive, never adequately satisfied, and is primary for TV watching, taken in its most general sense. More specifically, it fosters interest in suspense and mystery shows, quiz and participation shows, newscasts, and educational programs.

Cultural aspirations: When a desire is prominent to reach toward higher levels of social status, intellectual power, esthetic taste, civic responsibility, and executive mastery, then television is likely to be regarded very critically. If the medium is viewed at all, interest moves toward current events, educational shows, drama, sophisticated participation shows, and programs that employ whimsy, satire, or self-consciousness.

Success: The audience is constantly on the outlook for proof that it is possible to succeed, to win by the display of talent, to overcome obstacles, to reach a happy ending. Most television shows gratify this aim in one way or another, through defeating the villain, solving the mystery, clarifying the misunderstanding, or resolving the joke.

Variety: People look at variety shows; they also seek some variety in all the shows they watch. Where this is the basic aim, viewers usually emphasize relaxation and entertainment. They fight their ready impulses toward boredom and want items that will keep refocusing their attention without involving them too intensely or for too long.

Realism: Realism is the way in which more intense people and sharper motives can find their outlets without seeming immoral. It legitimates the violence of such a program as *The Untouchables* by using the guise of history and documentation and can justify almost any show. The logic is that it is valid for art to mirror nature—although audiences differ as to what is really considered to be realistic.

These and many other motives cohere into the particular patterns of each show, and in so doing sort out audiences. The movement of audience attention through time and from channel to channel responds to the array of symbolic configurations being offered. The flow of programs plays upon the audiences' interest with greater or less command depending on how aptly it combines, recombines, and projects human concerns and the means of resolving or contemplating them in fantasy.

CHAPTER SEVEN

THE TELEVISION
PANTHEON

The attractions of television have been described from many points of view, and many of its gratifications can be phrased in abstract terms and related to impersonal motives—education, culture, variety, and the like. These are undeniably important factors in television watching. When a viewer turns from one channel to another, he is searching among various systems of symbols to find those that will titillate, sober, inform, or relax him, using the format that seems fitting at the time. The purpose, the form, the subject matter, the plot, all are used as cues to guide audience interest and reactions. But all these flow through or are made manifest in the personalities, actions, and presence of television performers.

These people are the gods, major and minor, of television. They come and go, and who they are, what they are like, what they can do, are sources of intense meaning to television audiences. In this respect, television is an interpersonal phenomenon; it brings a stream of famous, provocative, talented, and unlikely individuals into the home, feeding an insatiable need to bask in the radiance of glamour, in the awe of skill, or in the enchantment of genius, to admire, envy, emulate, criticize, deny, or affirm the values represented by the performer.

These are not real social relationships; they have been

termed *parasocial,* to indicate their approximate nature. But the satisfactions they provide may be greater than those found in ordinary daily relationships. The audience gets caught up in knowing about the people who populate the television pantheon—to whom they are married, how they are doing in their careers, when they are or when they will be on the air. The viewers refine their appreciation to the point required to assess a particular performance in terms of their own sense of rising, sustained, or falling interest. Out of all this develop the peculiar qualities of what television demands of performers. This chapter observes some of the common stages in the natural history of careers, in television as elsewhere. It examines some characteristic symbolic configurations as these appear through particular television personalities and how they affect and select audiences.

By way of introduction, it is of interest briefly to indicate how viewers talk about television performers—the kinds of descriptive and evaluative terms they use, the degree of familiarity they reveal, and the intensity of feeling they display. The following two comments, obtained by asking viewers to comment on a long list of recently popular performers, reveal something of the many ways in which they recognize, evaluate, and identify with these stars. The first is made by a woman who clearly embraces TV.

> Brinkley and Huntley, I like them because they cover the world news and I like their personalities. They're just the kind of people who seem like someone you would know. Sometimes personalities on television seem like they might be friendly, not cold and inhuman.
>   Bill Cullen, on *The Price Is Right,* he's crippled in one leg. He's got a lot of personality; he's interesting. I like to watch the sort of thing where they bid on items. I really believe it because they're bidding and that means that they can't be fixed, like the quiz shows.
>   Then there's John Daly, on *What's My Line?* He has a lot of personality; he comes across to you just that way. I might

be disillusioned if I met him, but I just feel that if I knew him I'd like him.

Hugh Downs, of course; well, I don't think much of Jack Paar. It's not Hugh Downs I'm crazy about, but I like his show, *Concentration*. He seems alright but I don't know. I'm just not crazy about him, I just don't like him as well as some of the others . . . . I don't think Jack Paar is doing so well. I think he's sort of bust himself with his recent escapades. I don't know how, but I've heard people say he wouldn't last much longer.

Art Linkletter, he's a wonderful man; from what I've read I think he's a humanitarian. Like, for instance, if someone was missing, he'd have the wife on, or if someone was in the service, he'd have the wife and baby on and make a picture or recording of it and send it. I believe that he and his wife have several adopted Korean children.

Yves Montand gave a little performance on the Academy Awards. He was real cute. That is the only time I ever saw him, but I can't say I'd want to see more of him if he's just a song and dance man.

Desi Arnaz, when he was teamed up with Lucille Ball, was wonderful, but by himself I don't care for him. He just doesn't appeal; it was definitely the team that made them so good. She was really funny.

The second set of comments is made by a man whose attitude is that of the accommodator.

Edie Adams, quite a dish as I recall. I do like her although I seem to feel that I have seen too much of her. The last time I saw her it was in a big television spectacular and it was just the awfullest I ever saw. The show was no good, and as far as her part, if she wasn't miscast in that then I'm Rockefeller. I suppose that what she might lack in acting she may very well make up for in singing. I don't imagine I'll see her for a while, and I'm not too unhappy about that.

Gracie Allen, I'm sorry to say, but I never particularly liked her. She's off now and I feel that's for good, and I don't think I'll miss her in any way.

I just plain don't like June Allyson's looks. Lot's of men would love to grab her and squeeze her to death, but not me.

Lucille Ball is tops; she's TV's best and greatest comedian, Her shows are great; her styling is immensely entertaining. She's very attractive physically.

Ralph Edwards, I wouldn't walk across the street to see him. I never did like him. I'll never forget the time Lowell Thomas took the show away from him, poking fun at Ralph that just tore the show apart. Bret Maverick did the same to him, too.

At one time Arthur Godfrey was the top star of TV. I think he will remain in TV, but what hurt him so much in popularity was that he tried to hog the whole show. In the first place he's a redhead—there is either top or bottom for them, certainly no in-between. He must have made scads of money; what a terrific start he got in TV-land.

Groucho is the greatest ad-libber of all time. He can make a joke out of anything either said or unsaid. He surely does make it difficult for some of his guests. I hope he'll be around indefinitely.

Phases in Television Career

Broadly speaking, the theater, the movies, and TV are alike in their demands on writers, producers, directors, and stars, and durability and status in any of these media are basically similar in their origins. But TV is demanding in special and unique ways. It seems both more promising and full of opportunity and yet more fickle and potentially defeating than either the theater or the movies.

Television, according to the responses in our research studies, is less concerned with quality and more shallow than the other media. People feel that movies and the theater require greater basic talent and a more finished performance for success. The theater especially seeks to perfect itself and to repeat itself over long periods of time to particular audiences. The prestige accruing from a prominent role serves to keep a star in the limelight and alive in people's minds, and one or two movies a year may suffice to the same end. But television is transient and partakes of the nature of the passing scene. What it offers is thought to be quickly prepared, and certainly it is quickly displayed; a program has one shot in which to capture and hold a massive audience, and then it passes into limbo, with little opportunity for recall, re-evaluation, or repeat performances. Reruns, though they may be watched by sizable audiences and with considerable interest, can also seem as stale as last week's newspaper.

Television exposure is avid in its demands on talent. There are certain stars who hold their status and reputation on the basis of very few performances each season—Fred Astaire, Gene Kelly, Victor Borge are examples—but most have to rely on their capacity to hold the interest or affection of the audience through regular and extensive exposure. In this process, the biggest problem is that television personnel quickly wears out its welcome in the home of the viewer. Consuming people and material at a great pace, the medium puts considerable strain on performers' talents and on the creativity that can be made available. Furthermore, many shows and performers are intended by their sponsors to be suitable for all viewers, regardless of age, sex, or social status. Sometimes, therefore, television performers try to be all things to all people, without the central focus and meaning that attracts a smaller range of viewers who become the core of a loyal following. More generally, the problem contributes to one of the major dilemmas of television: how to reconcile high costs, special audiences, and innocuous fare.

We have already referred to the pronounced tendency of viewers not merely to accept what they are shown but to consider everything they see, including performers, in sharply evaluative terms. In connection with performers, this results in emphatic attitudes toward their personalities, special talents and abilities, idiosyncrasies and symbolic meanings. In these studies we also found that viewers were very sensitive to the public image of a performer, to the particular career phase in which viewers in general and critics now seemed to regard him. It was important to viewers whether a star was currently more or less popular than he had been, both absolutely and in relation to other performers, whether he was developing new talents more or less rewarding than the old, and whether he appeared to be ascendant or on the wane.

Our research showed that viewers' perceptions of and attitudes toward a performer's career phase are crucial elements in their responses to and evaluations of this person and his appearance on TV. Almost every performer is seen as somewhere along a developmental cycle, from just beginning, and on the rise, to an established plateau of varying durability, to a period of decline and then oblivion and (posssibly) resurgence. To most viewers it does not seem odd, owing to the transience of the medium, that fame comes readily and can fade out with equal speed or that performers should have peaks and valleys in their careers. This is part of what makes television a fascinating gamble, what makes its personalities attractive to watch and to identify with. It is enjoyable for the viewer to see when and how he must readjust his own preferences and loyalties to television and its people. In doing this, the viewer himself contributes to the rise, development, and fall of performers' careers, depending on the quality, intensity, and frequency of change of his attitudes.

The initial phase, the time that harbingers a career, begins when a new personality is talked about—by critics, in advertising, by M.C.'s, by established television performers who act as sponsors, or by viewers' acquaintances who happen to have heard of the new, prospective star. In this way, appetite is whetted; encouragement is provided ahead of time by some degree of social approval. The level of anticipation begins to rise, and this phase allows for testing in advance whether it seems likely that the new performer will be attractive, by noting who approves, what qualities are being emphasized, and on whose program the individual is to appear.

The real encounter occurs when the performer actually appears on television; thus begins the second phase, which can last over an extended period of time. With ability and adequate preparation, the encounter is usually auspicious, but it can be a troublesome moment. Novelty can be jarring, and the viewer is uncertain how much that is new should be admitted to his mind and how to evaluate what is presented. Exploration goes on, and the performer and his abilities become known to the viewer. Whether ultimately he likes or dislikes the new entertainer, he will often participate at the outset, if only out of politeness, deference to the source of introduction, or because of the commotion other people seem to be making. In the world of television and show business generally, it is hard to ignore an entertainer making a splash, even if one dislikes him. Part of the audience is likely to be antagonistic to some degree; commonly, the more vehemently the newcomer is being accepted and promoted, the more vigorously some negativists will join the audience in order to observe and to feed their resistance. Public figures who arouse this type of mixed audience include, for instance, Jack Paar and Zsa Zsa Gabor, in contrast to, say, Donna Reed, who probably has few watchers who "can't stand her."

The extent to which the new relationship moves onto a more stable plane depends on the degree and kind of recognition that occurs. Liking or interest are elicited when the newcomer provides a pertinent gratification in a style that holds attention. If these provisions are not recognized, the novelty may be spurned; it may have been adequate for a transitory moment, perhaps for a single viewing, but not meaningful enough for frequent experience. At the other extreme, recognition may be too great. The relevance of the performer or his evocation of the viewers' less accepted motives may be so overwhelming that the experience is either totally rejected or cannot bear repetition. Some talents have a largeness of insight so precisely or completely expressed that they can be tolerated only in infrequent doses. For instance, Danny Kaye or Jerry Lewis may evoke too many unsatisfied

childish impulses to be acceptable to adults on any regular basis, although the universal elements of their appeal may command vast audiences at intervals.

In the recognition phase, audiences usually develop a
sense of involvement and affirmation. The viewer feels,
"I like you," and his descriptive terms and feelings often
take on superlative and intense qualities—he's wonderful, terrific, a lot of fun, a riot; she's just gorgeous. During
this phase, the urge to associate with the performer may
be strong and sustained, or it may be controlled and mod-
erated in those whose needs are less intense or who hold
back in their interpersonal commitments. Such control
may be expressed negatively or ambivalently, as in the
phrases frequently used to describe feelings about TV
personalities—"I can take him or leave him"; "I don't care
much for her, but I'll watch her occasionally if the set
gets turned on."

From recognition, swept along on a wave of intensity
and initial overevaluation of the new friend, the relationship between viewer and performer may develop a
sense of intimacy, a feeling of mutuality. The audience
imagines that the entertainer displays an understanding
of their needs, which he reveals in his capacity to move
them, by the attention he gives to things they understand
or are pleased to have taught to them. "How funny! That's
just the way it is"; there is familiarity and comfort in
such a relationship. The new friend may seem "just perfect"; the audience hopes he will not change. This is the
moment of zenith, accompanied by a high sense of ide-
alization and suspension in time, classically underlaid
with fears and doubts that the situation can remain un-
changed.

These fears have good reason, of course, since such a
tumid situation cannot be sustained. As familiarity grows,
the emotional tone usually begins to moderate; the same
intensity is not required in order to know the performer

and what he offers, and fewer and fewer unexpected modes of revelation occur. Experience becomes more detached, more conscious, more available to intellectual examination and, potentially, to criticism. As the relationship normalizes by becoming fitted into routines and schedules, increasingly taken for granted, a continuing reorganization of perceptions is going on. The entertainer is now viewed as part of a context, no longer taking total precedence over other attractions but having to compete with them. The energies that rose to a peak subside to some degree and are redistributed in more diverse directions—toward other programs, talents, interests, or activities. In addition, people often become aware that, along with the gratifications they derive from a performer, they receive other, less desired attributes, and they begin to balance negatives against positives in the relationship. As doubts and competitors arise, the relationship reaches a crisis, a key phase between viewers and television entertainers.

Some relationships do not undergo this moment of crisis, or at least it is put off for some time. The long-lived entertainers of television offer central satisfactions by representing a significant aspect of human life in a vital way. They usually have a distinctive force and self-assertion that command attention and loyalty from the audience. While bland and mild characters can also gain recognition, their appeal will usually be brief unless it is accompanied by specific skills that lead to audience interest and gratification.

If the crisis leads to failure, the relations between audiences and performers usually do not permit revival. The audience turns away, sometimes gradually, sometimes suddenly, as their accumulated indifference finds alternatives. Television performers rarely manage to come back once they have lost their viewers. They may win a new audience through a change in style or a shift in locale (a fading TV comic might be enthusiastically received in night clubs), but the true comeback (the entertainer who is abandoned and later returns to renewed favor) is a theatrical fantasy, more celebrated in scripts than in real life. It is the entertainer's dream, to ward off his fears of oblivion. Symbolically, however, it is widely appealing as a theme, since it speaks of renewed potency, of love reawakened, of never really dying. When it occurs in any form, people can feel gratified. Thus they thrilled to Joan Crawford revitalized in *Mildred Pierce;* to Gloria Swanson in *Sunset Boulevard;* to Frank Sinatra, making the grade as an adult singer and growing in show business as an actor; to Buster Keaton for his funny commercials, etc.

Renewal sometimes come about because of a dramatic and revelatory experience and may be real and enduring. This may have happened to Red Skelton. The death of his son changed him from an ordinary comedian to a top clown; he gained a tragic depth, moving to a new and very human level of intimacy with his audience, who derived a more mystic sense of his talent. But the renewal of old, fixed ties may not occur in dramatic form; it may go on at comfortable, sporadic intervals; Jack Benny, Sophie Tucker, and other show-business ancients provide examples. In these instances, predictability is the important element, rather than inner or outer change. Their audience may not be great, because it is drawn from the constantly diminishing number who can muster the nostalgia and sense of history to pay comfortable respect to the institutionalized performer. The problem is that they are often granted remote homage, occasional visits, to renew the grandeur and marvel; but most of the time life goes on elsewhere.

Television careers, like friendships, are most enduring when stylistic change seems least relevant. That is, the more the entertainer rides on superficial representations, the narrower his audience and the more precarious his hold. His temporary success may be impressive as it rides the crest of some transitory popular interest, but it often fades quickly and is not renewed unless he can show a larger talent, an unexpected versatility, or unless he changes himself adequately to tap a deeper motif in society. With television audiences, there can be too much of a good thing; tastes and preferences mature and new learnings develop, as do new inner realities and new outer circumstances. Hence entertainers must decide how much they will grow with their audiences or whether to stick with the people who know them best; they must try to find the new motivations that are appropriate for each stage in their careers in order to gain a new group of loyal and devoted fans among TV's millions of viewers.

Performer Images and Their Symbolic Meanings

It is one of television's assets that it is able to offer an array of people and talent, each part of which provides a different symbolic value serving to define and to focus what is seen and to align it with certain audience groups. These symbolic qualities cover a wide range, but they form distinctive clusters by which the viewers identify particular entertainers. The symbols do not necessarily correspond to the type of person the performer actually is but rather to what viewers imagine him to be. They may always contain some elements of reality, but to a large degree they are produced in the viewers' fantasies of idealized images that come across in promotion, settings, introductions, and performances.

Thus, when prominent television stars are mentioned, a number of quickly identifying symbols usually come to the viewer's mind. Often the more concise and lively the identification, the more prominent the star in one's thinking, and these symbols sum up an image of the performer. Invariably, the symbolic values by which a performer is defined and evaluated pertain to his sex and age, his manner of relating to and the degree of intimacy with audiences, his talent (actual and potential), his career phase, the typical setting in which he appears, and something of his known personal life.

How do these qualities or features relate to the images and status of television performers? Many research studies have sought answers to this question. Members of the public have given information, both in their comments on TV personalities and in response to questions that sought to crystallize what seems to account for television success, in one shape or another. It will be useful here to present a few sketches of specific performers who represent different and interesting versions of stardom, to observe some of the general dimensions they present to the public via their particular individuality. They are examples available because of special studies we have made; other important performers could be cited, but they were not studied.

The Lofty Stature of Bob Hope

To have "arrived" and endured beyond memory in show business in itself confers a certain status and role in that business. There are a number of performers who seem above and beyond popularity, the size of their current audience, and even the reactions of the audience. These are the performers who have long and successful histories of acceptance and prominence, whose abilities are believed to be highly esteemed by other professionals as well. They are usually credited with having made important contributions to their profession, to society, to the armed forces, and they stand for much that seems professionally and artistically admirable and stable in the rapidly shifting world of show people. Their presence lends weight and prestige to the shows on which they appear, and these meanings are understood even though audience attention may vary.

Such people are the elite, through their unusual triumph over transience in public affection. In television such a triumph is complex and difficult. It means they have risen above the temporary nature and immediacy of the medium, to project a given quality or impression quickly, to be able to repeat it on call. Those who have proved capable of this are usually the legendary entertainers who do not seem to have more novel abilities on the TV screen than they had in other media. A prime example is Bob Hope.

Bob Hope is a familiar and accepted part of the American culture. In addition to his abilities as a comedian, he receives general approval for his all-American qualities of generosity and moral goodness. Few viewers say anything critical of him; unfavorable comments usually allude to a specific attribute or action of his that is disliked, but they are promptly qualified by general approval. It is important that viewers feel comfortable with him, and the over-all quality of a particular show in which he appears does not reflect on him or on his influence with his "friends" in the audience. That is, a poor show does not detract from Hope's reputation; there is a tendency to think of him as being "outside" the show and as being himself. This is an exceptionally well-developed image of stardom and one that comes to comedians of high repute more frequently than to most other types of entertainers.

Hope has a likable personality that appeals to a wide range of individuals. One reason for this popularity is that he laughs at himself, or at groups that don't matter (the Russians, for example), rather than at the audience and its failings. Also, he is judged "all-American"—sincere and well-meaning, a solid family-type citizen under a flippant exterior. Viewers typically feel that they know him well enough to be able to discount his lightheartedness. Rather, his comedy is a likable attribute, only lightly covering his sincerity and good deeds, such as entertaining servicemen in remote parts of the world. He is considered highly successful and undoubtedly very rich, but nevertheless a warm human being. Even feelings about his egocentricity (which is thought to be well developed and entrenched in his views of himself) are not detrimental, since it is assumed that he has a right to consider himself a strong and important person.

In earlier days, he often played the role of a white-collar "shnook," the confused cynic who lost girls to Bing Crosby and who still laments the "inferior" talent that never merits a real Academy Award. But as he has become a grander symbol of American wit, his bite has become sharper, his gags more acutely contemporary, and he has the comic elder stateman's permission from the public to find humor in the mere fact that he is "Bob Hope."

The Durable Clowning of Red Skelton

Another entertainer who has adapted himself to different media and found television audiences notably receptive is Red Skelton. Skelton is one of the most durable clowns in show business. He epitomizes a classic brand of slapstick comedy that has great appeal for many people. In its appeal there is, initially, a very strong element of attraction, along with some fearful, even ominous feelings, for Red, capitalizing on the various characters he has created, plays many aspects of the fool who gets himself into dangerous and absurd situations yet emerges unscathed. He is the duped innocent who remains uncorrupted by the world of sophistication, gimmicks, and complexity. Red is thought to be a simple and natural man.

People's feelings about his comedy color their impressions of his private personality. They believe him to be humble and forthright. They appreciate his efforts to give his all to them, his audience. His openness, his pleading to the audience to be with him and for him, forms a basic core of rapport. It sets him up as a somewhat sad, pathetic figure—the posture of most great clowns—who strikes an emotional chord in a mixture of laughter and tears.

He also represents the gay, whimsical, and youthful qualities of a clown. His gestures and deliberately erroneous diction are often calculated for purely playful effect. When he turns to the audience with a silly smirk or an absurdly contorted expression, he delights them, drawing them into sharing his childish trickiness. His comic roles have a primitive touch, relating them to circus and European clowns, or harking back to a time of less sophistication, when slapstick was more the rage and being "just plain foolish" was a freer source of hostile gaiety.

The Versatile Idiosyncracy of Victor Borge

There is an important level of show-business stature that implies greatness of transcendental order. It usually involves a range or degree of talent that people speak of with awe. Such entertainers may expose themselves less regularly than other performers. Rarely is anyone in a continuing series or in a weekly or biweekly show described in this tone of voice. Generally, people feel that if they were to see these performers too often they might not wear well. They seem to belong elsewhere, in some show-business circuit that comes around only once in a while. Among them are such people as Fred Astaire and Danny Kaye, and perhaps also Frank Sinatra, Ethel Merman, and Ingrid Bergman.

In a sense, these great artists demand too much attention, admiration, and concentration; they require a lot of

emotional space. Their performances are not part of relaxed television watching; seeing them is more like
watching a personal appearance in a live theater audience. Their talent often seems too distilled, too complex
and subtle, or too strong for a steady diet. An example of
these specialized talents is Victor Borge.

Borge appears as a friendly, human person—gay,
cheerful, and clever, capable of all sorts of tricks, and
amazingly versatile in talent and humor. He is a first-rate
musician and a first-rate comedian, a combination that
intrigues viewers, particularly in view of the fact that it
is a foreigner who combines these interesting abilities.

Borge's strength as a comedian derives from its self-
centered and narcissistic quality. This accounts in part
for the acceptability of his outspoken criticism and satiri-
cal lashing-out at accepted middle-class values. People
like to think that he can express the irony and sharp wit
which they themselves are unable to do—particularly at
values and objects that they also find important but
worthy of complaint or criticism. But for the same reasons,
and because of the intensity and rapid pace of his performances, he cannot be seen and enjoyed too frequently.

Borge's appeal lies in his ability to present music and
satire in such a way that it attracts people of different
levels of taste and sophistication. For working-class people he presents "art" in a way that they find acceptable
and not "stuffy" or over their heads. More than that, he
is able to come close to them, "down to their level," as it
were, by making fun of some of the generally acceptable
middle-class values. He becomes a popularizer of classical music and musicians by satirizing them; he is able to
gain the attention of this audience by expanding on their
familiarity with certain "ignoble" ideas about music.

His appeal for people of higher status lies mainly in
his versatility and his strong individuality. He presents the
sophistication of the "real" artist even while he provides

an avenue for people to laugh at art and the artist, setting himself up as the representative of both. By exaggerating the stereotypes of the performer or composer, or even of the music itself, he enables these viewers to laugh at themselves and their own emotional involvement with (for or against) such cultural expression. Some discomfort and uneasiness accompanies his performances, for the aggression and hostility in his humor contains ambiguities. His sharpness, his quick switches, his wit, as well as the more obscure appreciations to which he may be referring, at times make it uncomfortably uncertain who is the butt of the joke.

The Medium-Level Stardom of Janet Blair

Classifying individual talents must be arbitrary; careers are in motion, and at a given moment a performer may be in process of shifting from one level of stature or audience conceptualization to another. And some people are difficult to place because it is not clear into what category they fit. For example, we might question whether—given the diverse audience reactions found in various studies—Jack Paar is a theatrical marvel or a freak of public taste. But there seems little question about the reservoir of talents and personalities that people tend to call "solid." It includes singers with at least adequate voices, actors who know who to create a believable character, people who can be expected to turn in a finished performance time after time, year in and year out. It is this kind of performer who is the basis of the fundamental audience of television, a kind that wears well, that does not awe or require exceptional attention, admiration, or astute understanding. Some such stars are greater (Perry Como), some lesser (Teresa Wright), in the public mind, but the general sense they provide of theatrical authority and competence at a workmanlike level is apparent. An interesting example of an acceptably durable talent is Janet Blair.

Janet Blair's public image can be described as that of a capable, perhaps even first-rate, talent who has never attained the highest level of stardom. Viewers usually know about her varied career—on *The Chevy Show* and as Dinah Shore's replacement, in the past as Sid Caesar's TV wife, a singer with a band, a nightclub performer, a second star of *South Pacific.* Of her various talents, she is identified primarily as a singer, with dancing an added and important ability. Her record as an entertainer is defined as one of moderately increasing competence and reputation, but she is not regarded as having gained the independent pulling power that makes a performer truly "big time."

As for her personal qualities, she is regarded as pleasant, natural, and easygoing; she is someone who is easily liked, without affectation and not demanding of attention. There is a "girl next door" quality about her—lively and youthful, but not compelling or captivating. For all her pleasantness and smiling activity, she seems lacking in intensity, and, while people like her, they are not forcefully drawn to her. She does not communicate much sense of thrill or excitement, but, similarly, few people find her objectionable on any strong grounds. Janet Blair communicates a mature femininity, but she is not predominantly a "sexy" woman, and neither seductiveness nor passion are suggested by her demeanor and appearance. Her femininity has much good humor, even if it is not entirely free of sharp or challenging elements. Women do not consider her so glamorous as to overshadow them breathtakingly, and men do not think of her as remote or unapproachaable.

Of Janet Blair's talent, the most notable feature is her versatility, but she is not really outstanding in any one thing or even strongly identified with a particular style of singing. On *The Chevy Show* and as Dinah Shore's replacement, she comes across rather weakly as a mistress of ceremonies. She is thought to be not too sure of herself and not to have a firm hand on the proceedings of the show. These views are seldom stated critically; in fact, the audience tends to assume a moderately protective attitude toward her, they want to encourage her, and they often have a fair amount of sympathy with her position. She is praised as a "good team player," working well with others and not hogging the spotlight for herself; but this view tends to underscore her definition as a good supporting performer rather than a solo star, someone who perhaps can share top billing with another person but is not assertive enough to carry it alone.

Janet Blair exemplifies the entertainer who has attained a high level of recognition and popularity and who is widely acknowledged to possess solid talent and abilities but who fails to evoke strong reactions from audiences that would place her at the forefront of stardom. She suffers from limitations in emotional appeal and in definition, in that she does not present an easily perceived center of attraction. Her versatility works against her, in that it tends to diffuse rather than bring her into focus as a person. She remains on the level of being "pretty good in many things," an all-round girl who does not stand out in any one way and who thereby fails to reach the clear-cut identification or to obtain the strong emotional response that goes with stardom.

Tennessee Ernie, the One-Man Variety Show

The performers thus far discussed command a breadth and generality of audience. Their presence suggests only moderate orientation toward one or another specific audience, and to present them implies that a wide range of Americans will watch. A great performer (Danny Kaye) will get a special turnout; Skelton will draw out the more conventional, child-minded white-collar and working-class audience; upper-middle-class viewers will not want to miss Ingrid Bergman, etc.; but none of these will involve a sense of exclusion or an emphatic audience selection. Other entertainers, while well known, tend to have distinct appeals toward particular social subgroups, e.g., Art Linkletter, the Three Stooges, Mort Sahl, and so on. A less extreme case, but a clear example of a star with a wide but distinctly skewed audience, is Tennessee Ernie Ford.

Quite consistently, Tennessee Ernie and his show evoke a strong and generally favorable response from his audience. In large measure, this is because Ernie Ford is the show, regardless of what guests appear, what ideas are expressed, what entertainment is provided. He remains the fulcrum around which turn viewers' comments and reactions. He is a one-man variety show.

Remarks about the Ernie Ford Show focus on its liveliness, variety, range, and distinctiveness. These qualities pertain most to his personality and its dominance; he is spoken of as down-to-earth, neighborly, relaxing, sincere, and humorous. He turns his humor on himself and his own "unsophisticated" ideas and values rather than on others, and this gives him much of his distinctive style and creates a feeling of difference from most other TV comedians. It reduces feelings of hostility and adds to the impression that he is a humble comedian, folksy and unpretentious, someone who is well aware of and who can laugh at his own idiosyncrasies. But this also makes his warmth and humor seem narrower, to revolve too much around himself.

In his shows he follows a regular, predictable pattern —a combination of humor, song, and dance; foolish play and spirituals and unexpected bits of impulsiveness (which everyone knows will make their appearance sooner or later during the show). This contributes to the program's sense of variety, even though the format remains essentially the same from week to week.

A slight though significant undertone of discontent and

suspicion is encountered in audience reactions. Tennessee Ernie in this connection is felt to be something of a sham, appearing to be nicer than he actually is. His actions and his appearance are not perceived as complementary. He physically conveys notions of greater sexuality than his actions indicate; his aggressiveness is strong but muted. There may be difficulty in judging whether he is a singer or a humorist or both or neither, with opinions varying. It is not clear when he is acting and when he is "sincere"; one suspects a "country slicker" at work.

But Ford's obvious strengths and appeal are connected with these same qualities. He is regarded as multifaceted, a highly talented and skilled individual. He is considered serious yet jolly, down-to-earth yet sophisticated, a singer and a comedian, informal yet one who carries off his informality in a neat, poised manner. Because of this "depth" of personality, viewers find him an interesting entertainer, and these various poses, roles, and dimensions serve to hold people to his show.

Ernie Ford's appeal is, of course, quite general, but certain emphases are apparent. He has a special appeal for men; his virility, strength, and nonglamorous masculinity, and his particular form of earthy humor, anecdotes, and impulsive expression are found enjoyable. He is essentially a performer for adults; preteen-age children find him too adult and too sexually suggestive, and among teen-agers his material seems too dated, his songs too spiritual and "square." There are important differences along social-class lines; his show and his personality are especially attractive to working-class viewers. For them he seems both wholesome and entertaining; his shifting from impulsivity to slightly off-color jokes to a song from Broadway or a church hymn is found to be honest and earthy. They see Tennessee Ernie as impulsive, primarily along lines of sexual rather than aggressive expression. Lower-middle-class viewers have more mixed feelings about him and his show. They sometimes complain about his foolishness and find his humor unfunny, a bit too unrefined for their more controlled and moral manners. The upper-middle-class viewers in his audience respond to the role he plays, that of a shrewd southern hillbilly, and to his cleverness and skill as a performer, but in general he is less attractive to these viewers of higher status.

Walter Cronkite as An Eyewitness to History

There is no doubt that in the news and special-events field, just as in the entertainment field, the audience tends to build a relationship with a personality. People are attracted by the particular style, manner, and presentation of newscasters and commentators, just as they are attracted by these aspects of singers, comedians, and other entertainers. This is evident in the widespread popularity of Huntley and Brinkley. Having one man serve regularly, week after week, as "anchor man" or "co-ordinator" (or whatever term may be used for the person who represents the show) is therefore a desirable procedure in helping people to develop a sense of regularity about the program. This is particularly true when many public affairs programs appear or seem to appear at irregular intervals, since this makes it more difficult for people to be aware of them and prepare to see them.

For this reason, Walter Cronkite is a highly suitable person for his role on *Eyewitness to History*. Prior to coming to this show he already had a following from *You Are There* and *Twentieth Century*, and many people know him from his convention, election, and inauguration coverage. He brings many assets to his role. He is known as an established newsman; he is felt to be serious, responsible, and reliable, a man whose style communicates truthfulness. He seems self-assured without being vain, supercilious, or overbearing. He is judged to be well informed, interested in what he is doing, and capable of making people feel they are "on the scene" of what is happening. His calm demeanor is regarded as appropriate to his task; while his manner is somewhat formal and a few find him stilted, there seems to be little active dislike of him. He is considered a man who knows his job and who speaks to his audience with a vocabulary and syntax that are readily understandable, with a voice and diction that are pleasant. He does not generate the affection and warmth that Brinkley does or the controversies that Edward R. Murrow did, but then neither do most other newsmen.

Because of his association with *You Are There* and *Twentieth Century*, he has come to be identified as the man who takes his audience right to where things are happening. He is thus regarded not merely as a competent newsman but as a kind of journalistic historian, giving him a more authoritative role.

The Peaceful Morality of Roy Rogers and Dale Evans

A distinctive mode of success in the entertainment world is that which occurs through the "marriage" of partners. Some stars are viewed as part of a configuration; they are symbiotic personages who need to draw stimulation and sustenance from one another to achieve an integrated impact on the audience. There are television partners who seem to feed each other's success in vital ways and whose reputation seems to have evolved out of their partnership. Such pairs have been Louis Prima and Keely Smith, Sid Caesar and Imogene Coca, Lucy and Desi Arnaz. When these relationships are disturbed, the individuals often have trouble with their own careers; since they seem lessened, the magnitude of their stardom is diminished, their flaws are more visible. Caesar's problems with his timing become more apparent without Co-

ca; Jerry Lewis' appeal gets more childish without Dean
Martin; Desi seems to have no place without Lucy.

A television team that seems particularly to demonstrate the whole as larger than the sum of its parts is
Roy Rogers and Dale Evans. Rogers is thought of as a
former motion-picture cowboy star who now appears on
television and who, together with his wife, has succeeded in making a place in the general entertainment world.
His primary and traditional entertainment appeal is to
children and youthfully minded adults, in the form of
simple, direct, and pleasant cowboy fantasies, together
with songs and trick horses. He is a familiar old-timer
who looks amazingly young. He serves as a nostalgic
cowboy stereotype for many who enjoy him more for the
childhood memories he evokes than for his immediate
entertainment value. He keeps alive the Saturday after-
noons at the movies of one's childhood.

Dale Evans provides a spark for the team. Viewers
perceive her as a lively and warm support for Rogers.
She has an engaging and friendly smile, a bright and win-
ning way of presenting herself, and an ability to project
these qualities when singing. However, she probably
needs Roy Rogers to complement and bring out her own
personality. She seems more genuinely "folksy" and neighborly than does Rogers, projecting herself more as a "real"
person than merely as a stage personality.

The main element in their appeal is that they are plain
people who are believed to represent average Americans.
They are not thought of as tinsel show people, as entertainment personalities, as people solely concerned
with being successful. The Rogers are child-oriented and
have known tragedy. They are a type of Mr. and Mrs.
America, "like the people who live next door or down the
street." They are easily accepted as friends. They hardly
seem different when selling trucks in a commercial in a
realistic ranch setting, when singing songs on a show,

or, presumably, when at home without an audience.

They are folksy and homespun, with some hillbilly overtones. There is nothing unnatural or artificial about them, and there is no sophistication; everything is honest and down-to-earth. There is a note of responsibility about them, as part of their familial definition. They are clean-living and wholesome, reflecting, among other things, no need to emphasize sexual energy or innuendo. Thus, Dale Evans could become heavy and matronly without detracting much from her attractiveness, unlike other feminine stars whose careers rely heavily on their sex appeal. Much of the foregoing is symbolized by the expression, "They are good Christian people." A part of this means that they are countryfolk who have not been affected by modern urban values, styles, and modes of behavior.

Over all, there is little real identification of these two people with the cowboy world. They may be referred to in this way, but it is clear from what viewers say about them that they are not like the current crop of cowboys who dominate the television screen. Some people very specifically talk about how they are different from all the "other Westerns we see on television these days."

These qualities suggest how Rogers and Evans symbolize respectable and controlled impulses; energies channeled into moral, marital, and responsible directions; people who are rather passively entertaining. Their appeal centers on a childlike fantasy of a quiet and pleasant American West. Of course, for many viewers these qualities are too passive and too childlike, lacking in impulse and spontaneity, but the viewer can sit back and feel relaxed and comfortable—in fact, quite pleased with himself for watching this show. In doing so, he is adhering to a variety of moral principles that are specially meaningful to working-class viewers. The result is a broad audience in a cheerful, relaxed American mood.

Fred MacMurray as Fred MacMurray and
William Frawley as "Bub"

Another type of marriage in television is that of the
performer with his role. People feel that a great many
TV successes grow out of the fact that the actor seems especially well suited to the part in which he is cast. There
is a tendency to believe that this kind of marriage accounts for the success of Western stars, where the individual has no particular identity apart from the role
he plays. This has seemed true of Jim Arness as Matt
Dillon, Clint Walker as Cheyenne, and Hugh O'Brian
as Wyatt Earp. In other instances, performers do a sound
job in the series role but maintain distinctly separate
public lives as well. *My Three Sons* provides an instructive case of two performers with much previous show-
business background, both successful in their own ways,
who have joined in a TV series but who have quite different forms of integration with the program.

People remember Fred MacMurray from "way back
when" and in a wide variety of roles that they find hard
to recall specifically. Mainly, he seems like Fred Mac-
Murray, a light comedy actor of some merit, narrow in
range, a bit wooden in manner and appearance. He does
not seem to deal with much motion or emotion; people
do not feel strongly about him one way or another. He
seems basically "an ordinary guy," in itself a reassuring
show-business phenomenon. The viewers describe him as
pleasant and as wearing well, nice to look at, easy to
watch. He is neither an outstanding success nor a failure; he is not exactly a comedian or an actor; he does
what he does well enough.

He appears to wear equally well with men, women,
and teen-agers. He is not outstandingly popular with any
of these groups, but no one minds the fact that he was
given the lead role in *My Three Sons,* and most believe

he does well in it; with repetitive exposure many have come to be especially appreciative of his part in this series. There is some feeling that he is a bit too stiff, that he is "walking through his part" rather than acting a role. He can seem too remote and faintly amused by the role and the situation, playing it perhaps too much for laughs rather than for sympathy, identity, or realism. Nevertheless, these qualities are part of his idiom and give the audience a sense of comfort and ease in watching a familiar, ageless actor, secure in his craft.

William Frawley in his role as Grandfather Bub comes through as active and participating. He is remembered as one of the prominent and "lovable" characters from the *I Love Lucy* show. He is identified as an able performer and probably pretty close to being much like Fred Mertz in real life. He is well-meaning, at times obstreperous, at times vaguely ridiculous, now assertive, and then led by the nose by women and friends. He is not especially able or successful, but he goes cheerfully along in his comfortable fashion and manages to live an interesting and lively kind of life. Basically, he is moral and responsible. He does not have much authority or prestige, is a very average man, caricatured a bit in a friendly fashion. He is likable, uncompetitive, and affable in his argumentative way. He fusses and fumes, but his bark is much worse than his bite. He has many expressions and mannerisms that identify him readily.

The role of Grandfather Bub and the person of William Frawley seem to be made for each other. People are very fond of Frawley; they are glad to see him entrenched in a new role for which he seems so well suited. He brings considerable good will to the program. His presence can seem almost more pervasive than Fred MacMurray's, and he brings an elderly kind of identification to the show, both as a participant and as a sort of Greek chorus.

Pat Boone as a TV Star in Decline

Symbols, be they television personalities or of some other kind, have a life span. They are born, they develop and become mature, they live their entrenched years, and most of them age and perhaps die. The declining phase of a television performer, the period in his career when viewers no longer find him attractive and meaningful enough to seek out, is a special problem. It occurs at varying points in an entertainer's professional life, frequently quite early, sometimes after years of development, occasionally after many years of success. Pat Boone provides an instance of a television star who had a fast rise, followed by a sharp drop from the heights of success in this medium.

Boone was in a very real sense a Horatio Alger hero of television. Whatever the facts, the popular legend is that he came from a modest Southern family, that he appeared first on an amateur show and then on Arthur Godfrey's program and that soon thereafter success was his, and very rapidly. As a teen-ager he already had his own show. He married Red Foley's daughter, had four daughters of his own, and remained faithful and loving to his family. Among his many virtues are his deep and sincere religious feeling and his high moral quality. He is well educated, having attended college for several years, and he makes deliberate attempts at self-improvement. Thus, his appeal derived from his youth, his ambition, and his virtue, and there has been considerable wishfulness that he remain natural and unspoiled by success.

Everyone agrees that he is an attractive young man, that he has a pleasant smile that appears often, that he seems relaxed and informal most of the time, that he is especially gentle when he deals with or talks about women, and particularly understanding when he relates himself to teen-agers and teen-age problems. His talent lies in his voice ("He's a real singer, unlike many recent young singers these days"), which is pleasant to listen to. His show followed a set pattern, presenting one guest star whose talent is in Pat's area, a singer of some note. It was light and easy, with never anything shady or malicious about it, and Pat himself, no doubt, was believed to have seen to that.

His main weaknesses developed around his exaggerated goodness, his lack of underlying assertiveness and sexuality, the monotony of a bland show. These produced critical attitudes that developed as viewers came to be exposed to him more and more. His audience, even his most ardent fans, came to speak wishfully for more variety and color in his program and in his personality. As one teen-ager put it, "He is so nicey-nice" that his approach became boring, leaving many in his audience feeling saturated with softness and conformity.

The decline of this career is noted in the constriction of the audience groups to which Pat Boone appealed. Increasingly, with more exposure, it has become restricted to women, especially older women of the working class. He gained their interest as an idealized husband and tractable child. Men, particularly young and middle-aged men, see him as oversocialized, too good, too unreal, too unmasculine. Teen-agers find him more and more remote from their own world, too reserved, virtuous, "square," and in his moral tone much like the parents with whom they struggle.

Whether Pat Boone can appreciably modify his present image is problematic. He has, as of now, stabilized his image as the "good man" of conviction. He has fallen into the trap of an exaggerated attribute that limits him. His loyal fans may not consider this a limitation, but they are becoming a smaller and smaller group, and most other people do consider it serious. They are increasingly dissatisfied with the blandness he generates and the restraints and self-control he exhibits so directly, and as this satisfaction diminishes, his stature as a popular and attractive TV performer declines, perhaps to be pursued in another setting.

The purpose of these vignettes is to show how entertainers fit one or another cluster of symbolic meanings. They gain their audiences by exhibiting certain qualities and behavior that imply particular levels of capacity, skill, understanding, and personal meaningfulness. What the person is "really" like becomes transmuted into a public object representing specific ways of handling ideas, feelings, and appearances. These ways then have greater or less appropriateness for the time that they appear, whether hour, day, or era. This sense of appropriateness and immediate relevance to the viewers' needs for one or another kind of vicarious expressiveness is what ultimately governs the intensity, extent, and endurance of a performer's career.

PART FOUR

Television's Commercials

Television commercials are a lively and controversial subject; this is true not only for people associated with the television and advertising industries but also for the large group of viewers to whom these communications are directed. It is part of the accepted values surrounding the medium that one should have strong opinions about commercials, and, whether or not a person really does have strong opinions, he is likely to talk about commercials as if he has. Commercials are looked at, they do influence people, they are supposed to be watched with a critical eye and a suspicious mind—these facts all contribute to the abundance of ideas and feelings that people express when this subject is broached.

In this third and final section the many and often contradictory statements people make about commercials are sorted out and condensed, analyzed and assessed. Our goal is to formulate a few general propositions about commercials and about their relation to television in general and to its audiences. Three such propositions are offered, and they summarize the many individual ideas developed and discussed in more detail in the following chapters.

1. Television viewers think of commercials in much the same ways that they think of all television, of programs and shows, stars and personalities. They use the same descriptive phrases and the same modes of evaluation for both entertainment and commercials; they have many of the same feelings and respond in many of the same ways to the entertainment and to the commercial aspects of TV. In this sense, and from the points of view of the audiences, it is erroneous to think of commercials as something different and apart from other kinds of "communications" that appear on television.

2. Commercials are an integral part of a larger communications context, and this context strongly influences how people react to and what they get out of them,

what feelings they have about the products and brands advertised. In its most general sense, this context refers to all television and the feelings people have toward it. In a more specific sense, it refers to the show on which the commercial appears, the stars who appear on the program, the ideas and feelings that are a part of the program's image. All these factors influence the type and extent of commercial impact that is developed.

From another direction, the product itself has meanings and the brand has an image, and these provide an important context for the commercial. This determines in large measure the suitability of a commercial for television generally and for a specific program setting, and it affects the kind of reaction the commercial evokes among viewers.

3. Reactions to commercials, much like reactions to programs and personalities, are influenced by who the viewer is, the audience he belongs to, his social status, his attitudes toward the particular program and star context in which the commercials are shown. This means that a single commercial will have different meanings for different people, in much the same way that a single program affects different people differently.

These ideas about commercials provide a point of view for examining the many and varied opinions and attitudes expressed on this subject by television viewers. The details are presented in the following two chapters, the first focusing on viewers' feelings about commercials and the second on their understanding and appreciation of commercial forms and content.

CHAPTER EIGHT

WHAT IS A
COMMERCIAL?

Television commercials are a particular form of communication. They are a blending of cinematic techniques and selling messages, combining features that attract and repel in various proportions. They have a special character of their own, since they can combine the atmosphere of the motion picture, the cartoon strip, and the salesman on the doorstep with the particular setting that is television in the home.

This chapter discusses the special character of television commercials in terms of their distinguishing qualities. Viewers have developed expectations and attitudes that are not entirely the same as those they hold toward advertising in other settings. Within this framework, viewers distinguish different types of television commercials. It may be useful to describe some of these major categories, not being concerned with narrow technical considerations but observing the symbolic results of employing one mode or another in terms of how the audience reacts and how each approach reflects on the product or brand advertised. The chapter closes with some indications of optimal relationships among types of products, programs, and commercial styles.

174

The Uniqueness of Television Commercials

Commercials are advertising, and as such are considered by viewers as similar in purpose and meaning to other kinds of advertising. They share with other forms the basic function of informing and influencing people about products and brands. They are expected to attempt to modify feelings about a product and, hopefully, to motivate people eventually to buy it.

But there is a recognized uniqueness about TV commercials that derives from the special qualities of television. As do all media, television offers certain opportunities for advertising and presents particular limitations. These are known by viewers; if not explicitly and highly consciously, at least they are suspected and sensed. In either case, these unique qualities evoke reactions and are important determinants of viewers' feelings about commercials in general and of their judgments of the specific commercials they see.

Our analysis of how viewers conceive of and react to commercials indicates that for the most part these communications are "stories." What viewers mean by this—and it is not an idea they verbalize with any precision or with a great deal of ease—is that the commercial is a dramatic presentation. It has to do with a "human" theme that is introduced, developed, and brought to a climax or resolution. It hinges on some problem or conflict situation. It might involve several people, or it might have to do with a single individual, but always there is something that presses for solution and resolution.

Commercials are stories quite similar to the other stories that appear on television in program form, and, like these, they evoke simple, direct, condensed, and emotional responses. Viewers retain an over-all impression of what a commercial is about. The details are lost, collapsed into a summary evaluation and image of what they perceive to be the main ideas. This is how viewers describe several different kinds of commercials:

> Viceroy—their man thinks for himself. Usually the person is doing something other than his regular line of work and tells why he thinks for himself.

> The only thing about Coca-Cola commercials that I can remember is the tune. I don't know it, but I remember that is what it is. "The pause that refreshes." Something like that with the McGuire sisters singing it. I just like to hear those women sing.

> I like Mr. Clean commercials. They're kind of peppy. They are kind of attractive. I like them, the tune is catchy, I find myself singing that little jingle around the house.

> I become nauseated with the aspirin ads. It gets as far to the point of making you see swallowing an aspirin. These drug ads are not impressive at all. They show other brand names as Brand X and you're not supposed to know what it is. But you do recognize it. Dristan and Bufferin I'd say are pretty good [commercials]. They're more educational than the aspirin because they show you the inside of a person instead of just how an aspirin dissolves.

Most statements about commercials deal with their theme, the characters they use, and the mood they create. The theme summarizes the main idea: "Ivory commercials show them washing dishes and how it gets the grease," "The tinfoil commercial on *Maverick* is about protecting your oven," "Mr. Clean is a picture of a bottle that turns into superman who turns into a man who cleans everything around the house." Several themes may be perceived and the amount of detail that is recalled varies, but most commercials are collapsed into a brief summary idea that stands out as the story plot.

It is significant that viewers readily accept most themes, and they are not likely to quarrel about whether they are "good" or "bad." The exceptions have to do with sex or violence, and even in these instances viewers take offense only when the plots are too obvious and not softened or disguised by other materials. Sometimes they may wonder whether a theme is valid, but this response occurs more often in the abstract, when they are being critical of commercials in general, and less often when referring to specific cases. Over all, their response is dependent on mood and technique much more than on plot.

The particular technique utilized—and even more important, the manner in which it is used—is a major determinant of whether viewers will watch a commercial, what they will get out of it, and how they will evaluate it. They are very much aware of the different possibilities that television offers for using exciting and attractive modes of presentation. Exposition, demonstration, live presentation, case studies, announcers, sales pitches, animated figures, cartoon presentations, dream figures, magically changing products—these are but a few examples of the techniques that television uses and that viewers see as uniquely characteristic of this medium.

Perhaps most characteristic of television's mode of presentation is its ability to provide movement. "Television is alive" is a fairly common way people have of describing it. It is a more vital and active medium than are magazines, newspapers, or even radio. It provides visual presentations that need not—in fact cannot—be static. Several different kinds of movement are involved—movement over time; movement that reflects activity, impulsivity, organization, or randomness; two- and three-dimensional movement; movement in the sense of building up elements into new configurations or breaking them down—all done quickly, easily, magically.

Commercials invariably communicate a mood, something that sums up the main feeling of the communication. When people recall a commercial, it is often the mood that stands out in their minds: "It was a happy commercial," "I liked it because it is so peppy," "Their commercials show you how to do it," "I have to try to figure out what they meant by that one." These are examples of how people respond by feeling good, reflec-

tive, convinced, strong, excited, wondering, sad, or sharing in any one of the many possible attitudes that are
communicated by what is presented and how it is done.

Seen in a somewhat different way, television commercials rely heavily on feeling and affect to accomplish
their goals of informing and influencing viewers. Though
they often use a rational and logical format, reactions
occur in instantaneous, impelling, and emotional ways.
Fundamental to television's definition—and this applies
to its programs as well as to its commercials—are the
ideas of enjoyment, gratification, and pleasure; of indulgence, excitement, and fantasy. It is these qualities that
make commercials attractive, influential—and threatening.

The fantasy-producing power of a commercial is root-
ed in the visual picture it presents, its ability quickly and
subtly to change this picture, and its use of symbolic
modes of presentation. Imagery of this sort ignores reality and rationality; it is imaginative and magical. And,
because it can so readily develop the make-believe and
the fantastic, it arouses intense feelings, either pro or con.
Often commercials evoke responses in emotional ways
more than in intellectual terms. For these reasons they
are powerful in motivating viewers and in arousing all
sorts of fears and anxieties.

Another distinction of television commercials is found
in viewers' feelings that television advertising is expensive—even lavish—and in their attitude that commercials
should be well done, put together with imagination and
creativity, reflecting quality and providing entertainment.
These are beliefs that viewers hold of the medium as a
whole, most consciously about programs but also about
commercials.

Television is considered to be current and up to date;
at the flick of a switch the world is in your living room.
This view again carries over from programs to commer-

cials. It is especially apparent in connection with new-product advertising: viewers know that television is probably the best way to get rapid and wide-scale exposure, particularly on certain kinds of mass-appeal programs (Jack Paar is a current example, and Arthur Godfrey an earlier one). At the same time, viewers want a sense of immediacy in commercials. They have little tolerance for those that do not say something new and different or that do not describe something old in new and different ways. Many of the criticisms of repetitiveness derive from this point of view: a commercial that is repeated over and over again loses its feeling of immediacy. It strikes people as inappropriate to what television demands of its advertising. Television, in other words, provides familiarity with a product very quickly, and by the same process overfamiliarizes viewers with products in a relatively short time. This can be irritating, and the irritation is directed toward the commercials. Here, too, television affects responses to products as it does to programs and stars, creating a quick rise in popularity and then a rapid descent, caused by overexposure and its resultant fatigue.

Television creates the feeling that it speaks directly to the viewer. The communication is active and pointed: the newscaster is telling me about today's happenings, Dinah brings her show and guests to my home on Sunday evenings, Jack Paar is my friend, Ward Bond is my hero, *Father Knows Best* shows what happens in a neighbor's home that is almost identical with mine. Commercials are expected to partake of this immediate and active tie between the medium and its viewer. They do not communicate well when they are too generalized, overly abstract, too much directed toward "all" people. They need to be personalized in some way. There is appreciably less viewer tolerance for simple announcement advertising on television, although it can be effective in newspapers and magazines. TV commercials need to be specific in what they communicate to particular people— much as Jack Paar creates the feeling that he is a good-natured, friendly young man, who is nice to have around and who can be believed and trusted (or can he?) when he tells jokes or talks about products.

At the same time, television is a very public form of communication, and watching it has many social meanings. There is a large, simultaneous audience of which people are aware and to which they respond. This is basic to the morality that people invest in the medium and accounts for their insistence on talking about it in "good-bad" evaluative terms. The commercial, like the entertainment, needs to stay within the bounds of propriety and of broad public acceptance. Its visual and sensual stimulation cannot transgress certain limits (ill-defined and shifting though they may be), and viewers feel strongly that commercials should not stimulate them —and more pointedly, influence them—too much. Many of the feelings people have about the truthfulness of television commercials are related to the exposed and public side of television watching, as well as to the related attitude that it is a fantasy-producing medium that can easily and convincingly disguise and distort reality.

Commercial Types

It would be an error to think of commercials as narrowly informing and influencing, for this suggests too small a range of functions that they can perform and that viewers demand of them. They are also expected to explain, to prove, to demonstrate; viewers want them to entice, excite, motivate, and entertain. They feel that commercials should define and place the product into a context of personal meanings, aspirations, and a way of life. Even commercials of thirty seconds or less are "supposed" to communicate the total image of a product and a brand.

The essential point is that commercials need actively to stimulate the audience. There is a prevalent, if generally implicit, insistence among viewers that commercials be provocative in order to gain people's attention and to make them feel they are getting something worthwhile from this experience. Commercials, like shows, need to prove their worth, to use interesting techniques, to tell an engaging story, to say something new, different, and significant. They are obliged to personalize the communication so that a feeling can develop that special attention is being paid to individual members of the audience. If the commercials measure up to these expectations, then they will be watched. In many ways, the process is like an enjoyable game: catch me before I turn away; if you're good enough to do this, then I'll pay attention, be influenced, and perhaps buy what is being advertised.

There are many different types of commercials, and classifying them is often difficult. One type merges into another, and there are a number of possible variations of each type. Much depends on the particular techniques used, the mood set, the product advertised, and the program context in which it appears. In the following paragraphs, several of the more commonly noted types of commercials are discussed, indicating how viewers reflect on their main style, their appeals, and the products usually identified with each.

The product commercial can be thought of as representing an extreme type at one end of a scale that extends at the other to commercials that develop a richness of style and mood in selling the product. Product commercials are commonly thought of as sales pitches, with almost all attention given to the item being advertised. Usually, an announcer or salesman talks about the product and urges the viewer to buy it. These are the most stereotyped commercials on television, and they tend to be identified consistently in these ways:

> *The product dominates. It is the focus of attention, the main character of the drama. The format is highly stylized, beginning with a problem situation and immediately indicating how the product will solve it. Proof is often at a minimum, while urging is at a maximum. Broad claims are made, showing that this product is better than others or best. There is an apparent appeal to rational motives, an indication of easy if short-term solutions provided by the product, a stress of economy, and a tone of exaggeration surrounding the benefits to be derived from having it.*
>
> *The tone is aggressive. This type of commercial makes use of a pitchman, usually unknown and unknowable, with no real connection with the product. He is felt to be able to sell this today and that tomorrow with the same mechanical intensity, the same approach, perhaps the same words. He acts in an authoritative manner and stresses the need to act quickly and impulsively in order "to cash in on this good deal."*
>
> *It is repetitive. There is little attempt to relate this type of commercial to a broader context of program, announcer, imagery, or fantasy. More than any other type, it stands by itself; often it is a spot announcement. It makes its impression by being forceful and by having little variation. Product commercials of this type are thought to be the most repetitive on television, and they create a feeling that they dominate the channels, since they are seen at any time—on and between all kinds of shows, on every channel, at all hours of the day and night.*

Commercials of this type create the most annoyance and evoke the most criticism among viewers. They represent to many the worst in advertising that appears on television, and, for that matter, they often are felt to be the worst kind of advertising that there is anywhere. Viewers feel pressured and pushed by the more extreme examples. They resent the personal anxiety that so often is aroused by the salesman and complain about the distastefulness of the presentation. They grumble about the monotony caused by what seems to be constant repetition and about their feeling that these commercials interrupt the entertainment aspect of television.

The products that stand out as advertised in this manner are usually small items, sold at low or modest cost. They are thought of as spur-of-the-moment, impulsive purchases, something that a person is willing to gamble on once or twice. They often are personal products with which people experiment from brand to brand and find it difficult to settle on any single one with satisfaction.

These may be products that are openly defined as risky to buy; they do not need proper backing or assurances of reliability from an established and well-known business firm. Used cars advertised by small and unknown dealers are one example; inexpensive household furnishings also fit into this category. Soaps and detergents are commonly thought of in this connection, and undergarments and other personal grooming items are often mentioned. Perhaps outstanding among the items sold by this type of commercial are health remedies and those having to do with body care.

Commercials of this sort leave a heavy impression of a product name and a feeling of being impelled to act. Even in recollection, the evoked feelings may be unpleasant and tense, reflecting underlying anxiety. There are almost uniform objections to these commercials, but criticisms are more extreme among people of higher status, who are easily insulted by them and resent the pressure that is utilized. Criticism is voiced by men more than by women; the latter can be more intrigued by the chance of getting a good buy and of being able to try something out and also more willing to watch a brief, isolated commercial between their household chores. Older people sometimes find them informative, if not enjoyable, and they may respond to the problem-solving approach that is often utilized.

But, over all, commercials of this type suffer from their bold approach, the fact that they function in so blatant a manner, without benefit of known people and a known setting to soften their impact and to give them greater reliability and believability. They seem not to belong in any special place on television, so they stand out all the more. And, since they generally exaggerate the urgency and problem-solving character of their products, they easily arouse personal anxiety among the viewers.

On the other hand, product commercials are clearly successful. People complain heartily, but they do know about the product and not infrequently have bought it, if only on a trial basis. They also recall these commercials more than they think they do, and they probably watch and listen to them much more attentively than they will admit. Furthermore, they cannot escape these commercials, which are on so often and at so many places, and since they feel that they cannot escape them, they tend to accommodate to them—to give in, as if in so doing they can dismiss them from their minds. But the next time the commercial fits into the known pattern, the viewer has already seen it and now need not pay as much attention in order to have the message "drummed in" once again.

The product commercial, in sum, is effective so long as it deals with certain kinds of products. It can be damaging to others that require more explanation and more soothing imagery. It is tolerated well for inexpensive, impulsive purchases or those that deal specifically with problems pressing for immediate and quick solution. It is a type well suited to products that people do not really want to be identified with too closely or too openly, such as health-care items, and for which a moderately high level of anxiety will motivate purchase rather than work against it.

A somewhat similar type of commercial makes use of *demonstration*. It emphasizes rational appeals for the product, and, more than merely asserting claims, it provides a reasoned explanation and demonstration of what the product is like and what it can do. It seems an honorable and aboveboard way of advertising. It incorporates ideas of education and elucidation, and it is effective because it easily engages viewer interest and can tolerate novel and even provocative modes of demonstration.

Audience reactions will be governed by what the product is and how it is presented, but demonstration commercials in general have very wide appeal. They can be particularly attractive to more mature and reflective individuals, such as middle-class men and women who like to think of themselves as sensible and a bit conservative. But elaborate or clever forms of demonstration attract other kinds of people too, ranging in age from children to the elderly, of all status levels, though they have somewhat less appeal for the lower classes unless pointedly dramatic or magical material is provided.

The demonstration commercial makes excellent use of the special qualities of television. It relies heavily on pictorial presentation, on a convincingly rational framework in which to present and discuss the product, and on the medium's particular ability to transform (sometimes by magical means) wishes into realities. There are a large number of products that are well suited for this kind of treatment, and viewers can cite a long list they have seen advertised in this manner, including appliances, household cleaners, and foods. New products are felt to be especially appropriate for this kind of handling, because demonstration is regarded as useful for something as yet unknown.

Viewers distinguish between demonstration commercials that show how to use a product and those that show how it works. The former get consistently more favorable responses than do the latter, though not all the latter are criticized.

Those having to do with *how to use a product* are commonly thought to be appropriate for ideas for food preparation and serving or household items, such as appliances, cleaners, kitchen materials, paints, etc. Women are impressed more than men, particularly when they feel they are learning something new, but men may also enjoy these advertisements, even those about women's products. Kraft commercials are mentioned as exemplifying those that show how to use a product, and they are uniformly praised. Kaiser and Reynolds aluminum foil commercials come to mind also, as do those of Westinghouse, for these same qualities.

Upper-middle-class viewers talk about commercials of this sort as giving them new and constructive ideas that they can then pursue in their own creative fashion. They respond to them as stimulating and instructive, not merely to be copied but also as suggesting new ways of handling a product. For these people of higher status, the product becomes alive with greater possibilities. Lower-class viewers speak more often of seeing all the different possible ways the product can be used, of learning about specific things they themselves can do with it. They place little emphasis on creativity or the possibility of subsequent self-expression. These viewers are more enchanted by seeing what someone else can do, and their stand, unlike that of the higher-status person, tends to be quite passive.

These social-class differences do not affect the general appeal of "how to use" commercials, however. The widespread attractiveness of the type derives from the fact that these commercials show more than they tell. That is, they visualize rather than lecture and, in so doing, present an imagery that encourages fantasy: "I could do that too, it looks so simple and it comes out so good." The approach is calm, logical, and instructive; the motives it brings to the fore are solid and desirable. There is not too much suggestion of selling or influencing, and the pressure applied is hardly felt by the viewer.

In this connection, too, it is possible to detect how "education" is associated with TV and valued by its audience. There is a constant attempt to impose a factual, rational mode of expression on television, symbolized in education, and to diminish the emotional, exciting, spontaneous facets of presentation. Programs and commercials that somehow give evidence of emphasizing one more than the other find acceptance—as with adventure stories that people may find exciting but that also inform, or Westerns that incorporate scenes of violence but also have a clear-cut historical basis and a pointed moral message. Commercials of the "how to use" variety also provide this combination and are found interesting, provocative, and satisfying. They lose their effectiveness, however, when they become too pedantic, too educational. They need to remain dramatic stories, but with a distinct touch of instruction incorporated in them.

Commercials that deal with *how a product works* are different. Their emphasis is more on the product and less on the user or the benefits derived from using it. Technical factors loom large, and sometimes technical explanations do, too. Most viewers feel that this is tiring, especially if they sense that they really have to understand what is being said in order to get anything out of the commercial or if they feel that the explanation is being given by a trained person who is not technically competent.

At their best, commercials of this sort can be engrossing, for they too touch upon motives of explaining and learning, of being informed and making use of one's intelligence. The viewer can experience a sense of participation in an experiment or feel that he is witnessing a momentous and dramatic trial, the outcome of which is in some doubt. Crucial to people's reactions is the dramatic element that is present, and, if well done, it is likely to meet considerable interest and involvement. But, if poorly done, it becomes open to a number of possible criticisms, not the least of which is that "the commercial is fixed."

Viewers are of mixed minds about "fixed" commercials, and "fixing" is meaningful to most people only in the sense of referring to untruthful claims made in advertising. It hardly ever is an issue when a commercial is found interesting or enjoyable. It seldom is a consideration when the commercial appears on a show that the viewer likes, respects, and trusts. It gets mentioned mostly in an abstract, general way, indicating an over-all criticism of TV commercials, or it comes up in connection with certain products—health products primarily, but to a lesser extent cigarettes, cars, and soaps. In all instances, the reference is to exaggerated, unfounded claims, or to obnoxious and anxiety-provoking advertising.

> I can vouch for misrepresentation. I don't watch for that reason. Anything with a medical report, they aren't medical reports as such. That Cheer whiteness test. That's no good at all and doesn't appeal to the general public. How come that woman always picks the right stack? You know she would miss it some time. Why don't they show that?

Health-care commercials that use the "how it works" approach get consistent and universal criticism. Men are more critical than women, and higher-status people more than those of lower status, but these differences are slight, given the total emphasis on how bad such commercial are. Aspirin, Bufferin, and Dristan stand out in this respect; deodorant commercials are a close second. They are similar to the product commercials described above; the demonstration of how the product works serves to emphasize its utility but also proves to be an annoyance.

These commercials are convincing, however, for they dramatize a sales point and demonstrate visually the efficacy of the product. Annoyance derives from the personal discomfort people feel when bodily parts and functions are openly discussed, but the information provided and the manner in which it is given are instructive. The repetition of these commercials, which seems to be great, is bothersome, but the message does get across vigorously.

Commercials using announcers—and we refer here to those that use all kinds of personalities who talk about products—come in many varieties. They may be product demonstrations as well as highly dramatic or mood-setting communications. Also, announcers function in many different ways. At one extreme is the unknown, impersonal spokesman or pitchman, and at another is the well-known performer-endorser who becomes intimately associated with one product and its advertising (e.g., Dinah Shore). At least three other intermediate types stand out: the performer who also does commercials but does not become identified with one product (Jack Paar and Arthur Godfrey); the professional announcer who also acts and achieves performer status (Hugh Downs, Durward Kirby, and Frank Gallup); and the professional announcer who attains some degree of individual identity in viewers' minds but who remains an announcer (Joel Aldred, Betty Furness, and Julia Meade).

In general, the better known the personality and the more he seems to be a performer, the less criticism is directed at the commercial and the more apt the viewer is to watch it. This points to one of the main appeals of this type (and to one of the general meanings of all types of commercials): the more personalized the communication, the better it is liked. It then seems less like a commercial. There is, as a matter of fact, some evidence that viewers often "force" announcers to assume performer status so that what they have to say becomes pleasant and more acceptable.

Announcer commercials emphasize a communication process that is taking place between two people. It is built around the reciprocity that is assumed to develop,

and it creates feelings of social ties between the parties.
"He is talking to me and I should be courteous enough
to listen and watch." The better known the person and/or
the more personalized the message, the stronger this feeling will be.

Announcers also lend symbolic qualities to communications. They invariably speak with some degree of authority; even the "fake" doctors in the headache remedy ads
are responded to as if they might possess some medical
knowledge. Lower-class viewers are especially prone to
respond to such symbolic meanings, as are women viewers when they watch commercials advertising such products as food, household items, styles, etc. As a rule, known
announcers acquire more authority as they increase in familiarity among the audience. They become spokesmen
for the brand, much like Betty Furness with Westinghouse products and, to a lesser extent, Joel Aldred with
Chevrolet.

Viewers think of these announcers in fairly set and
consistent ways. They feel they know what kind of people the announcers are, and their known qualities strongly color the response to the commercials they present
and some of the feelings that become associated with the
products they advertise. Betty Furness, for example, appears to be a knowledgeable person, a woman who probably has combined a professional career with some kind
of home life (though this is difficult for viewers to figure
out), who is neither too sexy nor very attractive but who
is poised, calm, and logical. Her commercials are seen
as instructive but not very exciting; they are thought of
as being more for women, with men not too interested
in looking at her or hearing what she has to say. Aldred
is very controlled, a quiet spokesman suggesting underlying potency. He does not interfere with the communication, trying not to interject his own personality. He provides a setting for a commercial that suggests sincerity,

sensibility without extravagance, underlying power that can be called upon when needed, and a general attractiveness that is not outstanding but is appealing and easy to take.

The association between television stars and commercials is more direct: characteristics of the star, both apparent and symbolic, become associated with the product and with the specific commercial. In general, viewers feel that it is acceptable for stars to participate in a commercial, if only because this makes it seem less like an advertisement and more like entertainment. Their participation usually suggests reliability of the product, for the assumption is that a television star would not advertise something unless it were of high quality. The association of the star and the product is not taken lightly by either the star, the sponsor, or the audience; it is an important relationship that must uphold the reputation of the performer and the product and gain the respect and confidence of fans, users, and viewers. For these reasons, a performer who acts as an announcer tends to reassure the viewer as well as to catch his interest in the commercial.

On a symbolic level, other qualities are transferred from personality to product. In what are often stereotyped ways, a Western star makes people think of ruggedness, manliness, impulsivity, gratification, aggression, etc. Products like cigarettes, beer, coffee, autos, outdoor and sports equipment, are examples of products they think it appropriate for these performers to advertise. Musical comedy stars, both men and women, suggest more refined qualities and a higher status, even a touch of luxury. A light touch, running in the direction of greater femininity, is felt to be a common quality of these performers. Products that are thought to be especially appropriate for them represent, on the one hand, large investments and planned purchases and, on the other hand, foods, household items such as appliances, the more expensive personal grooming products, and those having to do with hobbies. Of course, in making these associations, viewers are very strongly influenced by what these and other performers now advertise.

It would, however, be a mistake to think of all performers as serving well as announcers. Much depends on the individual and the qualities associated with him; much depends on the product advertised and what will happen to it in this association. A great deal depends on the particular commercial in which the star and product are combined. In addition, there are some performers whom viewers find difficult to imagine as commercial announcers—or, more correctly, as having possibly a long-term and strong relationship with a particular product.

It seems more difficult for a serious dramatic performer or someone defined as an artist to serve as an announcer, except for the specific individual instance in which there is an advantage gained from the humor or shocking unlikelihood of such an appearance. Comedians are a mixed case in point: it is easy to feel that they make good announcers, most viewers can think of some who do appear in commercials (Hope, Skelton, Benny), and many can think of commercials with comic stars that were thoroughly enjoyable (Borge, for example). Some brands have built very felicitous associations with comedians (Jell-O, Johnson's Wax). But much depends on whether the comedian appears as a spokesman, an endorser, a symbolic figure, an integrator of the show and the commercials, or simply an announcer. There is always the question of what he is trying to do—whether he is joking or serious, insincere or sincere—whether he really cares about the product or is just doing a job. Since comedians are thought to be uncommitted people, their attitude often remains questionable.

Certainly, it is easier for viewers to relate to announcers whom they know and like as performers than to un-known personalities. But one of the problems associated with announcer commercials, especially when the an-nouncer has an identity of his own, is that the person in-terferes with the message. The performer comes to dom-inate the communication, so that the primary involvement of the viewer is with the individual and much less with the product and what is being said about it.

Viewers' reactions to this sort of involvement vary. Some appreciate it; the commercial becomes part of the entertainment, another opportunity to see a favorite TV personality. Others think that the individual interferes too much, that he gets in the way and blocks out other interesting information or presentations. Often those who take the latter point of view dislike the person ap-pearing in the commercial. The underlying question is how often a performer should be seen with a product and how intense the identification should be allowed to be-come. Viewers do not want this to occur either too fre-quently or too intensely. Performers should not be too commercial, and therefore they should not appear too often in this role. Their association with products is bet-ter tolerated if it is more general, less directly sales-ori-ented. A general connection—as Dinah Shore has had with Chevrolet, Ernie Ford with Ford, Perry Como with Kraft, Red Skelton with Johnson's Wax—is easier to ac-cept.

This discussion of announcer commercials must be qual-ified by what the person does in the commercial, how he acts, what kind of advertisement it is. There is a criticism of announcer commercials in which the performer "stands and talks," that is, in which there is little movement and much lecturing. Inactivity results in boredom, and, un-less the announcer is a favored star and an accepted authority, talk without drama and display can easily have the same result. Many stars seem too self-conscious when addressing an audience directly; comedians have an advantage here.

A commercial with a comedy star is not the same thing as a commercial with humor. More representative of the latter type is the *animated commercial.* It is widely known to television watchers, and with few exceptions it is enjoyed.

The animated commercial produces fantasy. It has many unreal and make-believe elements in it, and viewers easily relate to it, become engaged in it, and derive considerable pleasure and satisfaction from it. Its effectiveness often derives from the fact that it does not seem to be an advertisement—serious, pedantic, product-dominated, reality-oriented, attempting to influence and to sell. The humor implicit in the approach and explicit in the commercial itself disguises the motives of the message, or at least modifies them in such a way that viewers are willing to believe that the influence motive is not really present. To a large extent they do this so that they will be better able to enjoy what they see.

Animated commercials are thought of as the kind children like the most, the kind that are best suited for kids, the kind that adults really should not like or find interesting. But the animated commercial's audience is much larger; it may be more closely identified with children, but this only points to the nature of its appeal and the manner in which adults watch it. This is how adults talk about the type:

> Animated cartoon commercials would be for children's cereal, candy bars, most anything that children like. [Why?] Well, it's just that children love cartoons and they pretty much rule what mother buys in the food line.

> Cereal, bread, any product that a child could have an influence on buying would be suitable for cartoon commercials. Or, then again, beer and cigarettes have some very appealing cartoon commercials.

> My husband loves the humorous commercials. The bears in
> the Hamm's Beer ad are his favorites. Then the Burgie man.
> It's not too useful, but you enjoy the commercial as much as
> the program.

Animated commercials are usually thought of as short,
catchy, and to the point, and these qualities alone can
endear them to people. Their cleverness is appealing,
and so too is the sheer sense of enjoyment and entertainment they provide. Even when talking about them, people
evidence little of the defensiveness or standoffishness so
often found in connection with other types.

Mothers like to have their children watch animated
commercials. They think the liveliness is good for the
kids, and they can be pleased by the fact that these are
not "real" advertisements. They also enjoy them for themselves, more or less depending upon the product. Usually, serious and costly items deserve serious treatment and
are seen as inappropriate for this form.

Men accept this type of commercial readily for all
kinds of products, and in some ways they particularly
enjoy them for big, expensive, serious items. The Ford
cartoon gets mentioned occasionally; beer commercials
are talked about frequently, and usually as quite enjoyable and creative. "Mr. Magoo commercials" generally
are singled out for very favorable response.

Class attitudes toward animated cartoon commercials
vary somewhat. The upper-middle-class viewers appreciate the imagination displayed, and they can be very
conscious of the disguise of reality that is taking place
and still like it. Lower-middle-class viewers are apt to
stress their desirability for children, and much less directly for themselves. Lower-class viewers do not necessarily differentiate between children and adults except insofar as the product is concerned. Lower-class men are
especially appreciative of the cartoon approach.

Age is the most significant differentiating variable in

attitudes toward these commercials. Older people, over fifty, tend to feel uncomfortable about them, saying more emphatically that they are for children and not for adults. The strong identification of cartoons with children makes older people uncomfortable, although they might well enjoy a particular commercial employing this technique.

The animated commercial is in many respects an example of a much broader type, the *mood commercial*. This type is in sharp contrast to the product-oriented advertisement discussed first. Here the emphasis is on more remote imagery and surrounding emotions, with the product treated by display, by tone, by mode of presentation, more than by dwelling on its characteristics. By no means does the type ignore the product or its sale, but it deals with these issues in a different kind of emotional setting.

Mood commercials are quite common on television, and viewers have much familiarity with them:

> The most enjoyable is Salem with the bubbling stream and mountains and so forth, and the beer one that has the Swiss Alps. It's more or less relaxing backgrounds in a commercial. I like the relaxing music too, it's a change from all the hubbub.

> Well, I like the Coca-Cola commercial. I like the McGuire sisters and their singing.

> I like the Texaco ones because they try to keep varying them. They show the various ways they get oil for their tanker fleet.

Mood commercials are remembered as often offering music, singing, and dancing. They also are connected with highly dramatic episodes in a more specific sense than are television commercials generally. Quality production is assumed to be associated with this type of communication, as are other kinds of imaginative and provocative ideas. Viewers usually believe that such commercials are the most expensive to produce and that it is a sign of success and affluence to advertise in this manner.

Mood commercials are consciously acceptable to viewers, though not necessarily with the same degree of enjoyment or sense of entertainment felt about animated commercials. They are "soft sell," and, since the feeling of pressure is minimized (though not necessarily disguised), they do not arouse much direct criticism. Further, they are not usually thought of as repetitive, and there is an inclination to associate them with a specific program. It is usually difficult to think of a mood commercial as a spot announcement, though here too much depends on the product, and, when pressed to do so, viewers can recall examples.

The appeal of this type of TV advertising is that it stimulates fantasy. It presents, in entertainment form, a range of emotional meanings, definitions, and settings with which viewers can easily identify. The message is a bit vague, perhaps, but each audience member can easily feel that it has some relevance for him—if not in terms of the product, then in terms of the mood created. Annoyance is sometimes associated with the fact that it is too vague and therfore suspect, but, overall, this is a comfortable and acceptable form of advertising.

Audience reactions to the mood commercial depend on the product that is the subject of the communication. People who seek straightforward advertising and those who are suspicious of advertisers' motives, or those who seek assertive information and more immediate solutions to problems, will be dissatisfied. There may be some tendency for women to accept this approach more readily, but this is by no means clear. Social class and age factors do not seem to make much difference in viewer attitudes.

The mood commercial is successful in getting across a general image of the product and brand: Chevrolet's "The fun is in the going," Folger's "Mountain-grown coffee,"

"You expect more from Standard and you get it," and so on. An atmosphere is created that transcends product qualities, defining the product and brand in terms of richer associations and audience relationships.

This is the type of advertising for which viewers often express preference and the type they often say should be the only kind appearing on television. Just as the goal of television as a whole is often described as "education" —a loftly, pleasant, ideal goal—so, too, the goal for commercials is that all the "hard-sell," product-dominated, aggressive, and pressuring communications should turn into mood ads. In both instances the goal is an expression of an ideal and should not suggest that other types of commercials, like other types of programs, are disliked to the extent or in the way that people say. Neither should it be interpreted as meaning that the other types of commercials are not watched or that they do not provide stimulation or are not effective. Clearly, such is not the case; and the wished-for goal needs to be viewed as an expression of other kinds of concerns and attitudes that people hold toward television and toward its commercials.

In a similar way, the question of whether a commercial is liked or disliked, and in most instances the degree to which it is liked or disliked, is not the most relevant aspect of viewers' responses to advertising. Much more crucial to understanding their reactions are what the commercial is about and how it is presented, what is being advertised and where on TV it is shown, who the viewers are and how they feel about television and its advertising. In general, our studies of viewers' attitudes toward commercials do not reveal that product or commercial recall is directly related to whether or how much the commercial is liked or that commercial impact and influence is a result of this kind of reaction. The quality of the communication and its relation and appropriateness to the product being advertised and to the viewers to whom it is shown are usually the more crucial factors.

Commercials, Products, and Program Types

Television viewers associate products and commercials with different kinds of programs. In large measure their associations reflect what they have seen on television: if these combinations are not too jarring, if they appear appropriate and pleasing, and if they are seen frequently enough so that a connection is made, then they are acceptable. All viewers succumb to this kind of reasoning, and it invariably dominates their thinking in this area.

What combinations are made by viewers? A simplified ordering of some of the main ideas they express or imply follows, summed up as imperatives:

Current events programs: Commercials should be factual, without too much emotional appeal. Personalities should be kept to a minimum, letting the product "speak for itself," showing what it can do or demonstrating its usefulness. These programs should feature large, expensive items or those having to do with processes that the consumer does not buy directly but benefits from when he purchases other and smaller products. They may also feature products that require long-range planning or that are purchased more often by men for their homes, with infrequent purchase the rule.

Sports programs: Commercials should be lively, enjoyable, not very serious, impulsive and spontaneous, with known announcers or animated figures. Endorsements are successful, and they should have a masculine and a sexual tone. Impulse- and pleasure-dominated items are very suitable, such as beer, cigarettes, gasoline—and perhaps products like cars and household items, if not presented in an overly aggressive manner (and thereby cheapened).

Suspense-mystery programs: Commercials should not seem frivolous or demanding or interfering. In other words, strongly emotional approaches are thought to be distracting, and technical-sounding product commercials are thought to be too demanding of attention and too aggressive in tone to fit in well with this kind of program. Products that are masculine in meaning as well as those that are personal (perhaps products that are for tension release) seem "logical" for advertising here.

Adventure programs: A rather wide variety of commercial types appear suitable, ranging from product demonstrations to animated and mood communications. They can be both factual and emotional in their approach, and a tolerance for excitement and heightened feeling is apparent. Products can be of many kinds, though feminine items, both for grooming and for housekeeping, may be distracting or not well associated.

Western programs: These programs are a useful context for most kinds of commercial approach. Assertiveness, adventure, strength, and forthrightness seem to be especially appropriate tones, and products that offer gratification, that are easily bought and used, and that are directed toward men are considered to be especially well received in the Western-program setting. Cigarettes are a natural but overly common association, thus hampering individual brand identification.

Comedians: Commercials that provide relief from comedy are suggested, on the one hand, while those that make use of the comedian are readily brought to mind, on the other. Personal products of any sort are not especially good for comedy shows. Associations go instead in the direction of products that can tolerate some spoofing from the comedian or that benefit from the light and gay touch of a comedy context. Small-purchase items, such as cigarettes, are well suited to these shows; feminine items are felt to be at a disadvantage in this setting.

Dramatic programs: Product commercials are considered particularly offensive in this context. They are said to be too distracting and incongruous, forcing the viewer away from his set. Diverting, soft-sell, modified mood commercials are more appreciated or those with a known announcer, who talks gently and carefully about the product. Mood commercials that are too emotional might be distracting. Product types are not restricted so long as they do not demand too much thought or energy from the viewers.

Variety programs: Commercials that are quality-oriented are the most likely in this context, showing care, imagination, and creativity in preparation. Product-dominated commercials are felt to be very inappropriate, but demonstration, animated, announcer, and mood commercials are all considered suitable. Products, too, should reflect this orientation toward quality, and expensive and infrequently purchased items are felt to be suitable, especially if they do not require aggressive selling. Story contexts, family scenes, occasions, trips, seem useful to help organize thinking about the product in ways that are in contrast to the staccato pace of the variety format.

Situation comedy programs: Commercials that develop emotional appeals and imagery are preferred, though there is an acceptance of most types so long as they are not consistently aggressive or demanding in tone. The family definition of this kind of program makes it appropriate for products catering to men and women, to old and young alike. They should be "nice" products, useful, pleasant to purchase, found in every home. Food is especially appropriate in this context.

Quiz and participation programs: Commercials that make use of known personalities, including those appearing on the program, are felt to be best in this context. Personal endorsement is a part of the meaning of this format and is expected to be utilized in some direct or indirect fashion. Mood commercials are unusual here, as are animated cartoons. Emphasis is on people, relationships, and authority; products that are purchased on advice, on trial, for the solution of fairly apparent and not too complex problems, are most often thought of in this context.

Soap operas: With the mild exception of animated cartoons, most types of commercial approaches can be effectively utilized so long as they create the feeling of speaking directly to the woman. Products need to be feminine or in some simple fashion related to the woman's world.

What types of commercials and products should not be shown on what kind of programs? Viewers suggest few strict injunctions. They refer to what they believe to be extreme incongruities: beer and cigarettes on children's shows; personal grooming products on family shows, adventure shows, or variety programs; feminine products on mystery programs; serious, heavy investment purchases on casual amusement programs (such as sports); household items, such as soap and detergents, on Westerns, etc. Ideas are similar for men and women, higher- and lower-status people, young and old. The sexes should not be brought too close together by advertising men's products on women's shows or women's products on men's shows; sharp differences in mood should not be attempted, as with hard-sell and aggressively demonstrated commercials on dramatic presentations; television personalities should not allow "tainted" products on their programs, especially when they appear in or "near" the commercials; love stories should not have unromantic products advertised on them; and so on. As one of the viewers summed it up; "'Gas and love don't go so well together."

But even these ideas should not be taken too literally, for certain combinations of this sort are not in all instances rejected. There is evidence that the juxtaposition of seemingly incongruous commercials, products, and programs can achieve high impact and effectiveness through some deeper appropriateness. However, if not properly handled, when the contrast becomes too jarring, continued association can evoke viewer annoyance and protests.

From the foregoing it is clear that no simple or perfect correlation exists among commercial, product, and program type. Most programs can tolerate many products and several different kinds of commercials. At best there are only preferred combinations, but even then they depend on how the product is handled, what the specific commercial is like, what type of show it is. Thus, these are three interdependent considerations, and the effect of any commercial is invariably influenced by viewer feelings about the product that is the subject of the advertisement and the program setting in which it appears.

CHAPTER NINE

THE LOVE AND
FEAR OF
COMMERCIALS

At the outset, it is important to stress a point so often
denied, resisted, or reluctantly admitted by television
viewers: they have a great deal of familiarity with and
knowledge about television commercials. If a person
owns a TV set and spends even a minimum amount of
time watching it, he will know much about commercials
in general and about specific advertisements that he has
seen and to which he has listened and reacted.

It is obvious that there is a certain sophistication displayed in saying, "I don't watch commercials," and quite
a few people attempt to be fashionable in just this sense.
But denials are not necessarily forceful, and further
questioning—especially if indirect, not too challenging,
and connected with other questions about television and
television advertising—usually uncovers much information based on familiarity with these communications.

Patterns of Response to Advertising

Viewers are generally familiar with what is being advertised on television—the products and brands, the
kinds of commercials, the techniques and styles used, the
programs on which they appear, the announcers. They
are also aware more generally of the functions that commercials serve, the results that they are expected to

achieve, and what presumably makes for good television advertising.

Products and brands are most easily recalled, and the main way in which viewers identify commercials is by the subject of the advertising. A wide array of products and brands is fixed in their minds and quickly comes to the fore when the topic is mentioned. Sometimes they speak of a product without recalling a specific commercial since they assume that if they know the product to be popular they have seen it advertised. But, more generally, the name of a particular product or brand will call to mind specific commercials: Hamm's Beer and its animated figures, Post cereals and a slogan regularly repeated on *The Danny Thomas Show*, Chevrolet and Dinah Shore singing "See the USA." Viewers often associate particular types of products with particular types of shows, such as cigarettes, beer, and other "masculine" products with sports programs, detective stories, Westerns, and other "masculine" shows.

Commercials are also identified in connection with their particular show setting. The viewers know where certain products are advertised and are familiar with the kinds of commercials usually seen on a particular program. This mode of thinking about commercials is seen in the association of Chevrolet commercials with Dinah Shore's program, Kraft Cheese with Perry Como's show, Kellogg products with *Huckleberry Hound*, Winston cigarettes with *I've Got a Secret*, Tide with *The Rifleman*. They may also identify products with their commercial spokesmen, whether these are special figures created for the product, professional announcers, or TV personalities: ReaLemon with José Melis, Kleenex with Little Lulu or the Butler, electricity with Little Bill; Durward Kirby with Kellogg and Pittsburgh Plate Glass products, Betty Furness with Westinghouse, and Ronald Reagan with General Electric.

Almost anything that is said about commercials, whether fact, opinion, or feelings, reflects the extent and quality of the viewers' familiarity with them. It is important to recognize that they are most familiar to viewers in connection with some other aspect of the television experience—the products and brands advertised, specific shows, particular announcers or performers, the techniques used, the particular advertising style or format. They are rarely watched or remembered in isolation, but usually in a context within which the viewers recall what they are about and evaluate them.

Different viewers vary in their degree and type of familiarity with commercials. Children, for example, often have a most intimate knowledge, since their involvement with commercials is as deep and intense as it is with programs and they are much less inclined to deny what they have seen or to recall only part of the advertising message. Parents frequently relate how (and occasionally complain that) their children stay glued to the set while the commercials are on. This engrossment, permitting the viewer to recall in great detail what commercials are about, and this genuine enjoyment are not limited to children; they are also part of adult feelings and fears about television advertising and its potential influence. In this connection, too, the basic similarity between the show and the commercial comes to the fore: if the communication, whether entertainment or advertising, is felt to be directed at the audience in ways that can involve them personally in the dramatic presentation, the likelihood of their watching and enjoying it is greatly increased.

In general, women are more familiar with commercials than are men. Much depends on the products when making this observation, for commercials are directed at certain people—if not intentionally, at least in terms of how they are received—and women will be alert mainly to those they feel have relevance to their interests and goals. But almost all viewers make the assumption that commercials are directed more toward women than toward men, if only because women do much of the buying. The relationship of women with television and with advertising in general—namely, that it is a principal way for them to keep in touch with the large, out-of-the-home world—also contributes to their greater familiarity. Men, on the other hand, are less inclined to become absorbed in commercials; they watch them but do not always feel that they are relevant or pertinent to their personal needs and aims.

The higher a person's social status, the more apt he is to claim that he does not watch commercials, an attitude that closely parallels what the same people say about watching television programs. This attitude serves to limit their sense of familiarity with commercials, at least in contrast with the large number of television advertisements that viewers of lower status often recognize. But the type of familiarity these two groups of viewers have also differs, with a more exact understanding common among higher-status people, while individuals of lower status may be aware of only the main elements of the commercials in question.

There is much individual variation in these reactions, and to generalize oversimplifies a complex phenomenon. But the different ways in which viewers of different class levels perceive and understand commercials is not unlike the different ways in which they approach and react to programs. The upper-middle-class viewer is more selective, but also more active in his watching and understanding. Since people of this class level tend to share the protester's point of view, it is not surprising that they adopt the same position toward commercials, and, since responses to commercials are usually exaggerated, neither is it surprising that forceful criticism appears among this audience. They are impatient with what they (and others, too) feel to be an overabundance of commercials. They resent their persuasiveness. They are opposed to their emotional appeals, their seeming lack of believable arguments as to why Brand A is better than Brand B. They may wonder whether there should be any advertising on television at all, but this is an extreme and decidedly a minority point of view. More often, they call for less advertising, better advertising, and commercials that teach, inform, and explain.

Nonetheless, protesters can find much in television advertising that is satisfying and useful, and they are not all of one persuasion in their protestations and criticisms. The upper-middle-class housewife talks about those products she has learned about through TV and has bought as a result. The teen-ager cites the commercials he likes best, the humor of a certain advertising style, the appeals that are especially meaningful to people of his age. The executive who may criticize television programming can acknowledge the value of TV advertising and then in an expert (and still protesting) manner indicate what he believes to be "good" television advertising that "will really sell the product and bring the people in." Here, too, blanket criticisms do not succeed in drawing an accurate picture of what television advertising means to viewers who relate to television in this way.

In contrast, the lower-status viewer, who is often identified with the "embracing" stance toward television, watches more and therefore sees more commercials. He is less critical of what he sees, but he is also less active in how he watches and in what he gets out of the communication. His response tends to be concise and matter-of-fact; there is a literalness in his understanding of the advertisement, and typically he will not be imaginative about its subject matter. In this sense, too, his reaction to commercials is similar to his reaction to programs. For that matter, this difference reflects a basic distinction between the kinds of people usually found on these different status levels.

An even more important factor associated with viewer familiarity with commercials has to do with the imagined audience of the advertising—the people who are the intended recipients of the message. Viewers have strong feelings about this; their attitude is that most commercials are intended to speak only to certain people and not to all television viewers. This is reflected in the statement: "I don't watch a commercial unless I'm in the market for that kind of product." The assumption is that only people who have some interest in the product will listen and that others (and sometimes they are a majority) will pay no attention.

TV viewers think of the relationship between the audience and commercials, even more than they think of the relationship between the audience and programs, as highly selective, with certain people watching certain commercials and with most of them designed only for certain viewers. Though they may well exaggerate the selectivity involved, their view has considerable merit. It is based on the notion that commercials are a form of communication and that, like all communication, they should occur between interested, reciprocating parties. Since commercials have to do with selling and buying, the viewer should at least be expected to have a potential interest in buying the product.

One of the complaints that the viewer makes about commercials is that he has to sit through communications that "have nothing to do with me." He is irritated at the very fact that an ad appears on his TV screen, that it gets into his home and his consciousness when he really is not interested in it—or when he feels he does not want to be made interested in it. The owners of remote tuning devices believe they can control just this sort of thing.

One of our respondents talked about "killing the commercial," so as not to let it get to him. He got great satisfaction from doing this, and the control he thereby commanded made him feel he could be much more selective than the average viewer.

Most viewers do not feel as strongly as this about commercials interfering with their lives or impinging on their consciousness. If they are irritated, they walk out of the room, read a newspaper, or engage in some other activity for the few minutes an advertisement is on the air. Only a small minority will go to the extreme of purchasing a remote tuner, but their motives in so doing represent an attitude that is shared by a larger part of the audience.

The majority of viewers do not entirely ignore the commercials that they think are not for them, but they do modify the way in which they pay attention. They may switch from actively watching the program to inactively standing by. If the commercial is "good enough" to engage them, to make them interested in the story (if not in the product as such), they will become more involved and follow it through to the end. But if it fails to capture their fancy, they will follow it in a vague, inattentive sort of way, keeping tab on the flow of movement until the end is in sight.

Products advertised on television usually are mass-market items that may interest the majority of viewers. Hence, any sample of viewers will reveal a wide familiarity with most advertised products. But this should not hide or disguise the selective viewing that occurs and which viewers believe to occur. Women, for example, are thought to be more familiar with and more interested in commercials dealing with foodstuffs, household items, and personal-grooming products. Men resist these product commercials, and it is only when the advertisement itself is especially attractive (because of its theme, emotional tone, or special technique of presentation) that it succeeds in getting the average male viewer actively to watch it, to feel comfortable in so doing, and to acquire a sense of familiarity with what he sees. Conversely, men are thought to be more interested in beer, cars and car products, and shaving commercials; but this does not keep men from learning to hum "Pure coffee nectar, that's what's been missing," for example.

Children, again with the directness and candor so typical of this age group, are knowledgeable about those commercials that deal with the products they believe are for them or that make use of a technique they find to their liking. They may watch a particular program, feeling it is for children and enjoying what they see but ignoring the advertisements if they feel they have no relationship to young people. Attractive and lively techniques will gain their attention, however, and can make them feel that a product is in fact for them, or at least is something they can be curious about. Animated cartoons, generally assumed to be especially appropriate for children, probably function in this way. 7-Up commercials are cited as an example, but so, too, are beer commercials, and this sometimes arouses the concern of parents.

This kind of concern is characteristic of the reasons why viewers are suspicious and critical of certain types of commercials. When they are confronted with sly episodes or impelling themes that glorify the product, they may feel that it is not the product itself that is "legitimately" gaining their interest. They also realize that selectivity does not always operate as assumed or desired and that a viewer (whether child or adult) can easily lose control and succumb to the nonproduct appeals of an advertisement. These notions are intensified when applied to children, but they represent the concerns people have about the effect of commercials on all viewers.

Some Individual Reactions

We can best exemplify the reactions of viewers by citing excerpts from our interviews with different types of television viewers.

Consider, for example, Mrs. Brown, an upper-middle-class homemaker from San Francisco, whose approach to television is often one of protest. She is a woman of thirty-eight, the wife of an accountant, the mother of two sons aged four and six. She has a Master's degree in nutrition and is currently active in community affairs. In regard to commercials, for that matter in regard to television and a host of other subjects, she shares many of the preconceptions, makes many of the assumptions, and holds many of the attitudes of others of her social group, and especially of those who think of themselves as intelligent, well-educated individuals.

Mrs. Brown takes pride in the fact that her program tastes center on what she considers to be "quality" shows. They include *The Ed Sullivan Show* ("good entertainment; good, clean fun"), *Great Decisions* ("when it was on it was a fine show about our city and its problems"), and *Romper Room* ("the kids love the teacher, and it's a good preparation for school").

When asked about commercials, she immediately asserted that they really do not influence her purchase behavior or product preferences, and throughout the interview she made it a point to stress this fact. But she sees herself as different from most people in this respect; she assumes that other people are probably influenced by commercials and that she is not.

> I get information on new products in other ways, like *Home Economic Guides* and *Consumer Reports*. I would buy something I see advertised on television only if it's something I had a real use for before. TV couldn't convince me on anything. Just the opposite, in fact. But let's face it: people are susceptible to what they're told, be it political or commercial.

Mrs. Brown brings up an often repeated idea about commercials: they make you buy things you do not really need. She also alludes to an attitude that is expressed by many people: commercials not only fail to persuade one to buy, but they have "an opposite effect." This "opposite effect" is typically not made clear but, rather, is left to one's imagination. There is a threatening, even belligerent tone to these comments, but the underlying defensiveness is not hard to perceive.

Many viewers complain about the repetitiveness of commercials. It is, in fact, this characteristic, and their length and "misplacement" in shows, that emerge as the most irritating things about them. Mrs. Brown speaks in these terms:

> My husband finds them disgusting as I do. If you see a clever one occasionally, they'll work it to death, like Robert's Split Pea Anderson. Children find all commercials fascinating. Children love the repetition in anything. They like the known factor. It's necessary to constantly explain to them to make them see why I won't buy foods that are basically bad for them. You know, children are very susceptible to commercials, and sugar-coated cereals and candy gum which are harmful to children should not be shown on children's shows.

Mrs. Brown's notion that commercials exercise a strongly motivating force is apparent. She refers to this in typical fashion: they teach the children too many "bad" things. She thus shares a widespread tendency to project the influence of television onto other people, particularly those thought to be defenseless, innocent, and unsuspecting. Often this is the view that people have of themselves, and there is much pleasure to be derived from this passive stance, with a world of intriguing, exciting, good things arrayed before one's eyes on the television screen. The problem is, who is to screen out the attractive but harmful influences?

All in all, Mrs. Brown's view of commercials focuses on their pervasive influence on the individual, often contrary to his desires or needs and occasionally involving potential harm. She believes that more objective and respectable and individualized sources should be used for information. In her opinion, television should not be a guide to decisions, since its goal is to fashion behavior on an emotional, impulsive basis and not to provide information for a thoughtful and logical approach to activities.

Mr. Reilly, also an upper-middle-class person, holds similar views. He elaborates on many of Mrs. Brown's ideas when he comments on the sponsor's involvement with and relation to his programs. In so doing, he also expresses some of the insight and the well-articulated suspicion that often accompanies the protester's attitudes:

> I think that the sponsor decides what will be on TV because he has to pay for the time and he is interested in selling his product or his company to the public. Sometimes the network or local station may have to persuade the sponsor that a certain program will have the right type of appeal and audience for his product. The breakfast cereal people sponsor children's shows because they know the kids howl for their products and the parents buy them. Walt Disney sold Davy Crockett to the kids and he sold all kinds of Davy Crockett novelties and hardware along with it.
>
> I think the quiz shows proved that the sponsors were controlling the programs. They insisted that the programs and contestants be built up into national heroes in order to maintain audience interest, and it turned out to be a big swindle. The contestants were sold to the public as geniuses, and they were really actors who knew their lines. So this was a fraud. If their products were misrepresented to the same extent they would be out of business.

Not all upper-middle-class people hold such attitudes, but the tendency in this group is to be suspicious of commercials, to question the motives of sponsors, and to claim that they watch commercials—if at all—with considerable caution and a great deal of resistance.

The "accommodating" attitude, identified with the lower-middle-class group of adult viewers more than with any other status level, reveals more acceptance of television commercials. While in some fashion and to some degree these people express similar reservations, fears, and criticisms, they nonetheless find commercials lively and interesting; they see them as an integral part of television, and they tend to be more impressed by what they see.

Mrs. Hughes is a lower-middle-class woman of forty-five years who exemplifies in an exaggerated way many of the accommodator's feelings about commercials. She lives in Cincinnati and is the mother of four children and the wife of a funeral director. As with many viewers, she finds it easier to talk about TV commercials in connection with a specific show, in this instance *The Paul Dixon Show*.

> That's funny, usually I run out of the room when a commercial comes on. But with the *Dixon Show* I run in usually when there is a commercial on. Usually they have more fun doing the commercial than the program. They enact the commercial. If they advertise sausage, they actually fry a piece right there in the studio and get someone from the audience to eat it. I'll swear by them. I've bought almost all of the products and every one has been fine. They surely have lived up to their promises . . . . The *Dixon Show* is such a friendly, casual way to present items. It's like one big family; he makes jokes about it sometimes. He has a real swell personality. He really does put the commercial over. It makes you want to try it.

Mrs. Hughes participates with Mr. Dixon when he gives a commercial; he is pleasant to listen to, enjoyable to watch, easy to believe, and quite convincing. She feels that whatever is advertised on his show is worth trying, and her experience with the products themselves has supported this attitude. For Mrs. Hughes, the program and star context in which a commercial is presented is a crucial factor in her acceptance of the communication, and if she is able to identify a commercial in this way, her response is likely to include interest and favor. Only when she thinks about commercials without benefit of such a context does Mrs. Hughes, like most other viewers, become critical:

People don't like the interruptions on TV shows. All of a sudden a commercial comes on. I feel people would rather have the commercials before or after the program rather than the many interruptions. That Jack Paar! Every two minutes, if it isn't a commercial, it's a station break. That's awful.

Mrs. Hughes not only criticizes interruptions (and believes that other viewers dislike them); she also expects an appropriateness between a commercial and its show and complains when her expectations are disappointed:

Right in the middle of a romantic love story a commercial blurts out about gas and oil. By the time the commercial is over you're completely distracted from the story. Gas and love don't go so good together.

But none of this prevents Mrs. Hughes from admitting to the influence of television. She mentions it most pointedly in connection with her children.

The youngsters like the cartoon commercials, of course. They don't say anything while they're on; they just stop scrapping to look at the commercial. It's wonderful. They memorize it. And then after hearing it over and over I just unconsciously pick the product up as I walk through the store.

Later in the interview, she describes how television motivates her own purchase behavior:

TV advertising is good advertising; it's the best. If they acquaint the housewife with it so well on television, she isn't likely to forget it. I look at the commercials on TV and I go buy what they advertise. If it's on TV, I got it. When you see a product used or demonstrated you understand its use. Some products that I've bought are Bissell Sweeper, Dial Soap, Prell Shampoo, Gleem Toothpaste, aluminum foil for putting on the grill and then you don't have to clean the mess.

Mrs. Hughes accepts commercials and their influence on her more readily than do many other viewers, including women of her age and social status who adopt the same point of view toward television. By way of contrast, consider Mrs. Johnson, a woman of forty, mother of one child, the wife of an office worker in a large food chain. Her inclination is more critical, suspicious, and denying. She says that *Bourbon Street* and *Hawaiian Eye* are two of her favorite programs, and, when asked about the commercials on each show, she replies:

> I would be strictly guessing about who put on what. I always leave the room or file my nails so I don't have to watch. Oh, I guess Johnson's Shoe Polish sponsors *Bourbon Street,* The only reason I watched it is that it was a new gimmick, I mean the last commercial I saw. At the time, I was amused . . . . I thoroughly enjoy *Hawaiian Eye,* but so help me I haven't the foggiest idea who sponsors it. I bet you're sorry you asked me. I don't know why I'm so allergic to commercials, but I am. I get very busy when they come on.

Mrs. Johnson actually knows more about commercials than she first admitted, and as the interview continued she relaxed and talked about them in less defensive ways. For one reason why she dislikes commercials, she referred to the public nature of television and its advertising and to the sense of propriety and decency she claims commercials do not—but should—adhere to.

> They offend my dignity. People's personal habits are strictly that, personal, and the American public shouldn't be forced to view that stuff. A particularly offensive one is those statues, and they say males have sweat glands "here" and females "there." It makes me sick. I simply loathe the deodorants, dentures, headaches, Dristan, bras, and such commercials. They are so personal and I think the commercials intrude on my privacy.

"Intrusion" is a forceful way of speaking of a commercial's influence, but it is not an unusual way. Many of the complaints about commercials, and viewer's denials that they watch and are influenced by them, have this underlying theme: they speak too directly and too personally to me, and they arouse considerable anxiety within me.

The upper-middle-class viewer, to generalize about a large and diverse audience group, speaks of liking commercials that are strictly informative—that tell what is available, that demonstrate the features of a product, that adhere to an essentially rational and understandable format. He resists the idea of influence, and likes to deny that he is attracted to, excited, or induced by what he sees.

The lower-middle-class person—again generalizing—also says that "the function of commercials is to inform." But clearly these people are more fascinated by what they see. Indeed, they insist on being fascinated and are likely to accept more readily the exciting panorama of dramatic products appearing on their TV screens.

The upper-lower-class viewer assumes a more passive, less discriminating, and therefore still more accepting stance toward television as a whole and toward its commercials. He, too, will repeat the clichés about television, and he, too, will claim not to watch commercials and will imply that they do not (and should not) influence or exert pressure on him. But he is less critical of what he sees. He becomes more readily involved in what is presented to him, and his freer viewing stance allows him to sit back, relax, enjoy, learn, accept, and often try the product.

Mr. Strauss lives in Cincinnati; he is a twenty-eight-year-old clerk in a grocery store owned by his parents and is the father of an eight-year-old daughter and a six-year-old son. Without any hesitation, he talked about commercials on *The Rifleman:*

> It's Tide that sponsors it. They talk about the 25 boy scouts who come home with all the dirty clothes. They wash them in all different kinds of washers and all with Tide. They are trying to prove that it's the Tide that gets them clean and not the washer. They're just like all other soap commercials: they all claim their product is best.

Another program he regularly watches is *Alcoa Presents:*

> They have interesting commercials. They don't repeat them over and over. Alcoa makes so many different products that they can talk about different ones all the time. That keeps them interesting. I know that their products are good and they are very versatile in the many different products they make.

They have real cute cartoon commercials. [Give me an example.] I liked the one last week about the mailman and the man that was painting his house. The mailman brought this folder from Alcoa, showing how you never have to paint when you put on Alcoa Aluminum Siding, and that it's insulated. I think it does all they claim it does; also that aluminum is the up-and-coming product for low repair cost and upkeep; also the fact that it is so good looking and wears so well.

Mr. Strauss likes variety in commercials, and he repeated this idea (as did most viewers) throughout the interview. His approach to commercials is not unlike his approach to shows: they should engage his attention, they should entertain and stimulate, they should be interesting and exciting. And he will watch and listen—and be influenced to the point of believing what he sees and trying out the product. In fact, he gives the impression that he tries many of the products he sees advertised on television.

I tried Lestoil for removing paint from brushes when it first came out. But it didn't work for me. They showed it on TV and it seemed to work perfectly, but when you actually tried it yourself it was a different thing. Also Comet. It's very good, but still gritty. I brought it home because the wife had seen a commercial that said it wasn't gritty, so she wanted to try it. She likes it all right, but it was just as gritty as the one she had been using. The latest thing I bought is the one about the small tool that does everything. For $1.00. We had to have one of those, but we haven't found it to be nearly as good as it was shown to be on television.

The fact that these advertised products do not live up to what is promised (or what he expects) does not seem to trouble him, and it is evident that he and his wife enjoy learning about things on television. His buying is not done at random, however; he operates in a selective manner, purchasing what he believes he can use or needs. This is *his* control, and he pointedly stated: "I don't think anyone buys because of the commercial. They buy because they are in the market for the product." He later admitted that he sometimes buys out of curiosity, too—seeing something advertised, being attracted to it, and thereby being induced to purchase it. But he sees no harm in this; in fact, Mr. Strauss and his wife find it enjoyable, and if they don't like the product they just do not buy it a second time.

Upper-lower-class viewers readily admit to watching commercials and being influenced by them. They are least inclined to see conspiracy behind the screen, to conceive of sponsors' trying to manipulate the audience to do things against its will. They are more willing to take the sponsor at his word, to listen to advice from known figures of authority, and to respond to what they see in indulgent and spontaneous ways. Mr. Lester, a forty-year-old gas-station attendant, talked about Hudepohl Beer, which is advertised on the local baseball program:

> I like beer and their talk about it makes you want a bottle of beer. So I'll buy Hudepohl.... My wife tries things because Ruth Lyons tells her to, and anything she says goes. She really likes her. Do you? [to interviewer].... Durward Kirby does a real good job. He's a nice guy and can put it over good. I don't mind him. Don Wilson does O.K. too. He's good too. I like Peter Grant when he does commercials; he's an honest guy and I like him. I still like Durward Kirby for big-time stuff. The Chevrolet commercial is good for Dinah Shore's show. She's good looking and so is the Chevrolet. And Gary Moore and the Pittsburgh Glass Company go together and are done well. George Bryson does a good job on Hudepohl and they go together, baseball and beer.

But Mr. Lester sets limits on what should be advertised on television, and his views are representative of many others. He uses "children" as the deciding factor; they are symbols of moral standards that are felt to apply to adult society, too. They are used as a convenient and effective way of attempting to set limits on and to control the sensual meanings of television and the strong influence the medium can have on all people.

> I think those brassiere ads should not be allowed. I got kids

and it's embarrassing to all concerned. And the way they advertise cigarettes, it sounds like eating candy. Those ads gripe me . . . . I do think the kids are affected by commercials. They all try to imitate them. I just wish my kids knew their lessons as well as they know the commercials.

These cases illustrate the large number of ideas, attitudes, conflicts, and criticisms that people commonly express about television commercials. In general, the patterns of television embraced, protested, and accommodated are revealed in connection with commercials in much the same way that they are revealed in connection with entertainment. A viewer who is critical of programs and entertainers usually expresses a similar attitude toward commercials, just as a viewer who is inclined to embrace television's entertainment will exhibit the same approach to its advertising. There is a unity in television's content as it is perceived by viewers, and their response to its parts most often reflects their underlying similarity.

Criticisms, Quality Measures and Effectiveness

The stereotyped and repetitive criticisms that viewers make of commercials include these points:

> They take time from the show.
> They are overdone, overdramatized.
> They are exaggerated, distorted, untruthful.
> They are repetitive, monotonous.
> There is too much of a given product and/or brand advertised.
> They are too compelling, too exciting, too stimulating.
> They glorify unimportant virtues and values.
> They do not adhere to accepted moral standards; they influence and corrupt.
> They arouse personal anxiety about one's self, about one's social relations, about one's values.

There are too many commercials on television, regardless of quality.

Implicit in these criticisms is the idea that there is an etiquette of commercial communication, an appropriate way of advertising on television. There are standards that ought to govern what can be said and shown, how it is to be shown, how often it should be shown, where it should be shown—what is permissible, on the borderline, and beyond the pale. There is no fixed code, and viewers will shift in their attitudes from time to time, product to product, commercial to commercial, program to program. Nevertheless, the idea of a "right" and a "good" way of advertising on television is very much part of their feelings and is expressed in their evaluations of different commercials and commercial types and styles.

From the point of view of most viewers, as they subjectively experience television, there is a great deal of validity in all the criticisms. All viewers at one time or another become annoyed with commercials, and sometimes intensely so. They may also feel frustrated at the thought that aside from turning off or away from the set, there is little they can do to modify (let alone prevent) this annoyance. As a consequence, the experience of being "pressured" and enticed (and not infrequently of wanting to be pressured and enticed even while resisting this ensnarement) can carry with it a considerable amount of discomfort.

One response to these feelings is to deny that there is anything decent or valuable in television commercials. Criticism of this sort is a way of dealing with and holding off the overwhelming quality of the medium, both in its programs and in its commercials. Often what is involved is not such a simple matter as "I dislike the commercials [or shows]," but rather, "This is too much for me to handle and I want to get away from it." The resultant sorting-out process easily takes on a critical air, and criticism readily becomes the dominant response.

Criticism of commercials also involves people's inability to sort out the claims and influences placed before them. The more blatant the claim or the more insistent the influence, the greater the difficulty in determining the stance one should take: Should I believe it? Should I listen and watch? Should I buy the product? Is this one really better, as they say? Is this one best suited to my needs and desires? An abundance of commercials, especially if they seem similar and competitive, can lead to confusion.

There is little doubt that it is easier for viewers to criticize television in the abstract than in a specific context. That is, when talking about commercials in general—or for that matter, about advertising in general—a typical response is to express negative views. Sometimes these views are forceful and stated with a great deal of conviction; at other times they are more neutral in feeling, but the words are still critical. Such comments at times reflect a belief that all advertising is unpleasant or "bad" and that negativism is the proper attitude to hold and to express whenever given the opportunity. Men will do this more than women, and higher-status people more than these of lower status. But these are nuances; the over-all picture is one of negation and criticism when commercials are considered in an abstract, general way.

When people talk about commercials in a more specific way, much of their criticism fades away. Specificity here refers not only to individual commercials but also to particular techniques, to certain products, to announcers who are well known and appreciated, to advertisements strongly identified with a program and with a known style. Criticism also tends to fade away as one moves from urgent product-dominated commercials to mood commercials. The same tendency occurs the further one moves away from easily and impulsively purchased items, small and inexpensive products; there is less resistance to commercials that have to do with substantial, costly, and well-known products and brands.

Two important considerations are involved in these attitudes, and both have to do with the intensity of communication that potentially exists in television advertising. First, the more real, immediate, and intense the communication, the greater the likelihood that the viewer will respond in a defensive and critical way. Second, the greater the reassurance provided to the viewer in the form of familiar settings, styles, and figures, the less his anxiety, the more able he is to accept what he sees and the more likely he is to become involved agreeably in the communication. (How much he is influenced by the commercial message and whether he purchases the product advertised are only partly determined by these considerations.)

A commercial in this sense is a communication between two parties, one of whom is active and attempting to influence and to convince, while the other is listening and accepting what is being said and shown to him. This is the defined relationship, and it is a *social* relationship, in which the two parties are thought of as having obligations to each other. Each has expectations of what the other wants and will do, and standards of morality and propriety implicitly govern what is done and what is not done.

The viewer is thought to be under an obligation to watch and to listen, to allow himself to be influenced about what is being said, to the point of buying the product. And viewers commonly do fulfill their side of the "bargain"—they watch and listen, they allow themselves to be influenced. If for some reason they do not, they are inclined to give an excuse ("I have so many things to do in the house that when the commercials are on I just do them") or to protest defensively ("I just won't look at those things; they're all very bad").

The viewer feels that the advertiser must uphold his end of the obligation—to inform, stimulate, excite, involve, please, and entertain—all without transgressing an invisible and shifting line that marks off what is proper and acceptable from what is not. When in this relationship the viewer feels that he is being dealt with unfairly —when the commercial is too harsh, manipulative, aggressive, unpleasant, or anxiety provoking, or when the product is made too attractive and easy to buy—resistance is likely to come to the fore and to be expressed as protest, anger, irritation, or discomfort.

A commercial communication is not limited to the explicit form and content or even to the symbolic meanings of what is being said and shown. As in ordinary face-to-face meetings between people, other considerations enter and influence the outcome. Probably the most crucial of these is the context in which the commercial appears— the placement it has in time, theme, and mood in relation to other things shown before and after it.

A context serves as a lead from the entertainment to the commercial, by holding attention and then shifting it to a new stimulus. It provides an emotional setting, too, and it is in these terms that viewers associate certain kinds of programs with certain commercial approaches and products. By and large, the stronger and more favorable the context in which a commercial appears, the less criticism it arouses. If the program and personality context are liked, there is an increased likelihood that the commercial will be liked. There is also an expectation that programs that are "good" will have commercials that are "good," especially if they have been associated with the program for an extended period of time.

A context helps viewers to identify a certain style of advertising (*The Chevy Show* is a good example of this) and prepares people for what they will see. It often serves to make the advertising more acceptable. Sometimes the context itself takes on the character of a commercial, as Dinah Shore and *The Chevy Show* have in some respects done for Chevrolet. And the context persists in people's thinking, since even after a separation has occurred they will continue to think of a particular show or star in connection with a product once identified with them.

Viewers not only see commercials in relation to programs and personalities but also force these associations on them; they make the commercial more acceptable by placing it in a known and supporting setting. Standing by itself, with little connection with what came before or will come after it, a commercial can seem threatening and unpleasant. In a known setting, it is softened because it is endowed with some of the qualities of the people and themes thereby associated with it.

None of this is meant to suggest that all commercials require a setting or, conversely, that all commercials should attempt to minimize the influence of the context on the communication. Much depends on the goals of the advertising, the kind of setting one is considering, the nature of the product, the type of approach being used. All these factors are interrelated in complex ways. Some product commercials, it seems, cannot tolerate a program context and do much better when standing by themselves. Conversely, some programs cannot tolerate product commercials. Medicinal and other health remedies are a case in point: they can probably be advertised usefully in spot announcements. Also, commercials that are very much identified with a specific program can take on a boring quality of sameness; there is not enough newness and excitement about them, and people are less likely to watch.

Today's TV audiences feel expert about commercials and invariably proceed to evaluate them. Embracers, accommodators, and protesters alike, of both higher and lower status, will talk about photographic technique, the use of symbols, the quality of production, or the fact that a certain product is advertised in a consistently attractive and recognizable style. In some instances it appears that the commercials on a program are evaluated in place of the program, and perhaps they operate not only to advertise a product but to draw off negative feelings that might develop and otherwise be directed at a program or its stars. Here, too, there is a close relationship between the entertainment and the commercial aspects of television.

This relationship makes its appearance in still another way: television is regarded as a commercial enterprise. Entertainment, pleasure, fun, and relaxation are only surface manifestations of this medium, and at the core of it are people who invest large sums of money and who expect to get a return on their investment. These are the sponsors, who buy television time, pay for shows and entertainers, and more or less willingly underwrite all kinds of wonderful entertainment. But just as with any other kind of business enterprise, sponsors are not thought to do this out of the goodness of their hearts. They expect a return in the form of the purchase of their products. They present shows, but they also present commercials, and if the first are obviously intended to attract viewers and to entertain them, the second are obviously intended to inform and influence people about their products.

The commercial side of television—that is, its sponsorship—is probably more prominent in people's understanding of this medium than of any of its competitors. People can think more readily of magazines and newspapers apart from their advertising than they can of television; news and editorial content are more likely to dominate their understanding and attitudes. And in these media, advertising can be more easily ignored, overlooked, and dismissed; in television, advertising is more intrusive and compelling.

In this same vein, viewers do think of television as getting them to respond to its commercial aspects. While they might not like to admit to TV's general ability to influence them, they almost always point out how it has succeeded in getting them to purchase certain products. Sometimes this happens quite quickly and easily—"It's just something that we tried out"—or somtimes it occurs after long exposure to advertising. In the latter instances, the viewer will usually point out that "we needed the product, and it wasn't just the advertising that made us buy it." This is an important qualification, for it suggests how people dislike the thought that they are motivated to do something against their will. They prefer to believe that they use TV advertising in a selective manner, learning from it and then making use of it in terms of other personal considerations.

In conclusion, one implication of all this is that commercials are actually experienced in a much more integrated way than is suggested when criticisms are elicited. Both embracers and accommodators seem relatively little moved to spontaneous criticism unless extremely provoked. They feel that they get something from commercials (as do even some protesters) and that these are part of viewing television, of supporting the medium. Seeing commercials and reacting to them is part of being a consumer of both television programs and the products offered with them.

APPENDIX
ON METHOD

Of the sixty-nine studies that provide the information on which this volume is directly based, fifty-nine were done in connection with specific television programs, two were studies of proposed TV shows, seven were studies of television performers, and one was an extensive research of attitudes toward television conducted in 1960. In this appendix we present information regarding these studies, indicating in more detail their objectives, the research methods and procedures used, the sample plan followed, and examples of interview schedules and questions. We also present several summary descriptions of the populations interviewed in these investigations.

While these sixty-nine studies are most closely associated with this volume, Social Research, Inc., had also conducted a number of other studies of television and its programs and people, beginning in late 1940. For example, in television's very early days a series of documents was prepared on the social and psychological meanings of TV and its newly emerging definitions and attractions. From time to time during the 1950's, studies of individual programs, stars, and commercials were undertaken. All these materials contributed to the thinking of the authors of this volume, even though the research data and findings were not directly used here.

Specific Program Studies

The fifty-nine studies included in this group are heavily weighted in the direction of variety shows, reflecting the interests of Campbell-Ewald Company, the sponsor of these investigations. Eleven studies were made of the Sunday evening *Chevy Show* starring Dinah Shore, the first of which was done in May, 1958, and the last in December, 1960. Eleven other studies pertained to *The Chevy Show* when it featured other stars and performers, and in some instances when it took a form other than its usual musical-variety format.

The Pat Boone *Chevy Showroom* was also a program of interest, and five of these shows were studied between June, 1958, and October, 1959. Five additional non-Chevrolet sponsored musical-variety programs were the subject of inquiry during approximately the same period.

Other programs that were studied included five Westerns (*Wagon Train, Stagecoach West, Bronco, Bonanza*), seven adventure stories (*High Adventure, The Islanders, Route 66*), three current events-public affairs shows (*Eyewitness to History*), three dramatic presentations (two with Art Carney, and "My Three Angels" on *Ford Startime*), two *Chevy Mystery Shows*, a situation comedy (*My Three Sons*), and six musical-variety programs in which a well-known personality, most often a comedian, was dominant. These six shows featured Fred Astaire, Victor Borge, Red Skelton, Bob Hope, Steve Allen, and Danny Kaye.

In all these studies our immediate objective was to determine how viewers reacted to the show, its personalities, and its commercials. These were the most obvious kinds of information we attempted to collect, both for the assessment of the individual show and for purposes of comparing it to previous shows in the series and to other television programs we had studied. In addition to these viewer reactions and evaluations we also wanted to learn why viewers reacted in this particular way. To this end the interviews made use of other kinds of questions in order to get at more general knowledge of and feelings about types of shows, performers, and commercials; manners of watching programs and commercials; and other material reflecting broader attitudes toward television.

The sample population for each of these studies was 200 people, approximately half of them men and half women, all over eighteen years of age, who had watched three-fourths or more of the particular programs being studied and could be reached by telephone. Qualified viewers for each study were found first by asking whether the particular program was watched and for how long it had been watched; a third question checked for the sort of knowledge of the program that would indicate the viewer had watched it at least three-quarters of the time. In the few instances in which nonviewers were sought, an appropriately similar screening process was followed.

At the early stages of this research series, we faced the questions whether telephone interviewing would provide a sample adequate for the study requirements and whether the information obtained in this manner would be suitable and valid for the analysis and interpretation that was to be made. Our previous experiences with telephone interviewing had strongly suggested that the interview results would fulfill the requirements of the research and that adequate coverage could be obtained, since about 80 per cent of the urban population is accessible by this mode of communication. Nevertheless, the first few studies included face-to-face interviewing, and systematic comparisons of interview results from the two types of approaches showed no consistent or important differences in response. Periodic checks, made during later stages of the research, supported this conclusion, so that the large majority of interviews was conducted by telephone.

All interviewing was done by groups of local interviewers, starting immediately after a telecast and being completed within seventy-two hours. To obtain a random selection of respondents, a controlled procedure was developed, one that interviewers could easily follow and that would insure a routine and constant selection process. This was deemed important so that representative reactions to shows would be obtained and for purposes of comparing the results with other television survey research and with findings from one study to another. An interview validation program by the local city supervisor and by our own supervisory staff kept constant check on the selection process as well as on the validity of the content of the interviews.

The selection procedure involved the preparation of a series of "random rulers" that corresponded to the number of column listings on a telephone-directory page for a particular city. The ruler was cut to varying lengths for each of the columns; a ruler used with a four-column telephone directory in Denver, for example, might have its first column cut to 17.0 centimeters, its second column to 5.5 centimeters, its third column to 24.7 centimeters, etc., these lengths having been determined by a random procedure. Each interviewer in the city had a different ruler, and periodically the rulers were called in and replaced.

By placing the ruler on any directory page (these pages also being selected from a list of random numbers), the interviewers had a series of telephone numbers immediately above its cut edge. Their instructions were to call the first five residential numbers immediately above the cut edge in the first column. If no interview was obtained from these numbers, the interviewer was to go to the next column and call the five residential numbers above the cut edge, and so on. If an interview was obtained from any page, another page was then selected from the random-number list and the procedure repeated. In this way, no more than one respondent from those listed on any one page in the directory was interviewed. As each list of directory pages was used up, it was replaced with another.

The interviewer kept a tally of all calls, showing how many were dialed, how many were answered, and how many resulted in a completed interview. These tally sheets, returned with the completed interviews, made it possible to determine the proportion of viewers to non-viewers. This information proved a sensitive measure of the popularity of a particular program at the time. When base lines for these measurements were obtained, it became possible to see which shows were attracting and holding an audience.

After the first few studies, it seemed desirable to use different forms of the same interview schedule for any single study. This allowed us to use a more varied group of questions, to focus more pointedly on special areas of interest, and still to have a sufficient number of responses for the research analysts to remain confident of the results. We eventually settled on five forms, four of which were heavily quantitative and structured in their approach, while the fifth was essentially open-ended. All forms contained a series of demographic questions—age, sex, education of respondent and head of household, marital status, and occupation, and, for some shows, the number of people in the household, the number of children in the family, organization membership, car owned and car-purchase intentions. This information provided a basis for classifying the interviews and making initial analyses and interpretations.

An example of a typical interview schedule may provide a better indication of the approach used and the specific information collected. After obtaining various kinds of personal and social data, the four structured questionnaires would ask: "What did you think of this show? About how often do you watch it? How did this show compare with others you've seen in this series? If you were to rate this show, would you say it was excellent, very good, good, fair, poor? Why? Who sponsored the show? Who were the people on it? What two things on the show did you like best? Why? What one thing did you like least? Why?"

Specific questions designed to get at the quantity and quality of commercial recall were included, such as, "How many commercials were shown? Tell me about the commercials. What do you remember about them? What did they show? What did they say? See if you can be more specific. What did they tell you about (the product advertised)?" Frequently, very pointed questions about different aspects of the commercials, their content, participating personalities, technique, or theme, were asked either in open-ended or semistructured ways.

Regarding the show, questions often took this direction: "What parts of the show did you like best? Describe them. Why did you like these best? Which parts of the show did you like least? Describe them. Why did you like these least? What are your feelings about (the show, the star, the acts, etc.) this season? What seems to be happening with it? What gives you these ideas?"

A series of paired word choices were asked about the show and the commercials; for example, "Thinking about the show, was it unusual or ordinary, uneven or even, red or blue, exciting or relaxing?" A similarly structured question was, "Who would have liked the show best, a man or a woman, a fun-loving person or a conservative person, an engineer or an artist, someone mature or someone youthful, you or someone else?" Sometimes the same type of question was asked about the product being advertised, and often there were more general, unstructured questions regarding the product, its presentation in the commercials, its relation to the program being studied, and the stars who appeared on it.

The open-ended questionnaires covered a more diverse number of topics and encouraged a freer kind of response; they included fewer questions that could be answered by declarative statements or clear-cut alternative responses. A more or less typical schedule made use of these questions:

1. What did you think of the show? What was it about? How would you describe it? How did you like it?
2. What parts of the show stand out in your mind? What parts did you particularly like? Why is that? What parts didn't you care for too much? Why?
3. How did this show compare with others you've seen? How did it compare with others that had the same idea in it?
4. Some people say they can't tell one guest star from another these days. How do you feel about that? Why? What's your opinion about seeing guest stars on this program? Why is that?
5. Which scene on the show made an especially strong impression on you? For what reason? Which guest made a particularly strong impression on you? Why?
6. What are some of the thing you would have liked the star and his guests to do on the show that they didn't do? Why would you have liked those things?
7. Let's talk about the star. What did you think of him—the way he looked, his performance, the things he did on the show? What did you especially like about him on last evening's show? Why? What didn't you care for too much? Why?
8. What kinds of shows would you like him to have during the next few months? Describe them for me—what they would be like, what he would do, who would be on the show, and so on?
9. What about the show when there is no main star on it, how do you like it then? Why?
10. What other television programs do you know about that are on at the same time as this one? Name them for me. Why don't you watch these other programs?

11. How does this show compare with other TV programs? What program is it most like? In what ways is it better than other TV shows? In what ways isn't it as good? Why?

Questions regarding the commercials and the product advertised followed the same pattern:

12. What was your impression of the commercials on this show? What were they like? Describe them for me.
13. Which commercials did you enjoy most? Why? Who else might enjoy them?
14. Which commercial was the most informative? Why? Who would be most interested in a commercial like this? Why?
15. Which commercial was the least interesting? Why? What was wrong with it?
16. There was one commercial for (a product). What do you remember about this commercial? What did it show? What did it say? How did it make you feel?
17. What did the commercial tell you about (this brand)? What kinds (of different brands) are there? What are they like? What are their special features?
18. What does their slogan have to do with the product? Where else have you seen the slogan? How do you like it?
19. What does the slogan mean?
20. Why do you suppose (the company) sponsors a program like this?
21. How would you go about buying (the advertised product or the brand)? What would you do? Where would you go? What kind would you buy? Why?

The five interview forms were each used with about the same number of respondents. Analysis would typically begin with the necessary coding of both structured and unstructured responses. Our greatest analytic emphasis was given to an examination of the open-ended responses. This was done by several research analysts, each attempting to view the interview material for their social and psychological implications. We were interested in the meaning of what was said, in the tone of response, in the implicit attitudes and understandings of the viewer, in the information the interviews contained about the respondent and his relations to the program, the performers and their performances, the commercial messages and symbols.

Both the tabular and the qualitative materials were looked at in terms of who the respondent was—a working-class housewife, an executive of higher status who said he did not like television, a newly married man who worked in a factory and was in the process of setting up a household, an older person who watched a lot of television, a person who considered himself a devoted fan of this type of show, and the many other possibilities that we constantly encountered. It was in terms of these kinds of analyses that we found it valuable, even necessary, to think of television as having several distinct audience groups, and to look upon programs, performers, and commercials as systems of symbols which these different viewer groups related to in unique and always personally meaningful ways.

By way of summarizing our description of this type of study, some data on the population contained in our samples are enumerated in Table 1, appearing at the conclusion of this appendix.

Personality Studies and Program Pilot-Film Tests

Two studies of pilot films were undertaken, both for program series that later were scheduled for regular television viewing. The purpose of these studies was to review the specific program and the type it represented for its basic themes and meanings, the public reaction to its main stars and characters, the types of people to whom the series would and would not appeal, its potential audience growth, and its compatibility with a particular sponsor and product. In one study the sample was 126 men and women and in the second, 119; in both instances, individual and group face-to-face interviewing was done. In both cases, sex, age, and social-status characteristics were filled on a quota basis. The results of these two studies, in addition to providing the information for which they were designed, contributed to this volume by suggesting how television viewers respond to new types of shows and the manner in which definitions, expectations, and evaluations of such programs are formed.

Seven personality studies of three different stars are included in our total of sixty-nine inquiries. The purpose of these studies was to learn the then-current attitudes toward these stars, to determine what the main determinants of these attitudes were, and to find out in which direction and at what rate they were changing. To accomplish this, it was found important to ask about many TV personalities, so as to be able to locate and then to assess viewers' feelings about the stars we were immediately interested in. The line of questioning followed in these studies, which made use of personal, face-to-face interviews, usually began with what programs the viewer watched and his knowledge of and attitudes toward different performers, and then continued with specific probes about the personality, the career, the abilities and talents, the past and the future of the star(s) in question. Projective devices, including picture stories, incomplete sentence stems, and make-believe episodes were utilized as a means of helping people talk freely about these individuals. The results of these researches, together with the information collected on television performers from other types of studies, contributed to our knowledge of specific personalities and, more important, to our understanding of the underlying processes in terms of which viewers relate to, identify with, and evaluate TV people.

A summary description of the samples for these nine inquiries is presented in Table 2, at the end of this appendix.

The General TV Study, 1960

A single general study was conducted during the first eight months of 1960, the results of which are used extensively throughout this volume. It was designed to provide an overview of the then-current attitudes toward and uses of television. As described in the original memorandum that outlined the research, the broad goals of the project were four in number:

1. To determine how the public views current television offerings and to assess what changes and shifts are occurring in public attitudes toward this medium, its programs, personalities, and commercials.
2. To obtain information about specific shows and people at the height of the 1959-60 season in order to give guidance for program evaluation and selection for the coming television year.
3. To provide a more complete understanding of the meanings and appeals of different program types, making use of the numerous television studies we have done for Campbell-Ewald during the past two years, together with data collected in this investigation.
4. To indicate as best as possible what seems to be the important emerging trends in people's feelings about television as a medium for entertainment and advertising.

These are some of the specific points we want to provide answers to. Our approach to the study, however, will be more broadly based; in this sense our goal will be to explore in detail the social and psychological meanings of television as a medium for entertainment, advertising, and communication.

The sample for this study was 255 persons, selected on a quota basis from nine different cities, all by means of face-to-face interviewing. The quotas, as filled, included the following: by sex, 125 men and 130 women; by marital status, 204 married, 15 single, 8 divorced or widowed, 28 children; by social status, 50 upper middle class, 111 lower middle class, and 94 lower class; by age, 32 less than twenty years, 100 between twenty and forty years, 102 between forty and sixty years, and 20 over sixty years. All were television-set owners, and one-third of the sample owned more than one set.

Because of the diversity of topics we wanted to cover in these interviews, and because at the same time we were obtaining certain kinds of information in our regular series of studies, different interview forms were used with different categories of respondents. Most of the interviews took between one and two hours, and each of the eleven different forms had a somewhat different focus. The different schedules were not used simultaneously; the results from the initial guides were reviewed and assessed for purposes of designing subsequent ones. In other words, we incorporated what we learned in the early stages of the research in the design of the later stages.

The initial research schedule was quite broad and general in the topics it dealt with, beginning with a series of questions about the respondent's family, how they spend their free time, what they like doing individually and together, how other people they know spend their free time, why they and others do these things, how these patterns of leisure-time activity have changed over the years, how leisure time is thought of in relation to older people, younger men and women, and so on. The schedule then moved on to a series of questions about television, though the previous questions almost always evoked many comments about the uses and meanings of television as a leisure-time activity. The more specific probes on television included these:

How important is TV for you? About how much time do you spend watching television on weekdays? on Saturdays? on Sundays?

How many sets are there in your household? What kind(s)? Where are they and why?

Think back to when you first got TV. When was that? Why did you buy the set in the first place? How did you feel about it then? About how much time did you spend on it then? What were some of your favorite programs then? Why those?

What were some of the things you used to do in your free time before you had TV? What happened after you got TV? How did you rearrange your time?

As we moved on to more current viewing practice, the respondents were asked:

What are some of your favorite programs now? Why these? What TV programs don't you care for?

Generally, what would you say has happened to television in the fifteen years that it's been around? What do you suppose is likely to happen to television in the next ten years or so?

Think ahead for the next couple of years now: what kinds of programs will be most popular? Who are some of the women stars who are likely to be most important? What will happen to Westerns? What will the TV specials or spectaculars be like?

Who are some of the men stars who are likely to be most important? What kinds of information or educational programs do you expect to see? Why?

Will TV become more or less important for teen-agers? Why?

Which programs may not do so well? Who are some of the TV stars who are likely to be less popular?

The concluding questions of this first interview guide provided the respondent with a series of assertions about television (such as, "Television has been one of the most important influences on American life"; "Unless they improve and clean up television, the government will have to step in"; "Television is the best kind of entertainment; it completely absorbs and relaxes you") and asked him to comment on each of these in terms of his own views and experiences. In all interviews (in the subsequent series as well as in the initial ones), a variety of personal and social questions was also asked. Twenty-six interviews were collected with this schedule. The information they contained was analyzed by the research team; very little was done in the way of tabulating the frequency of responses, except for those questions that referred most directly to "how many" or "how often." The sample was too small for this kind of review, and our intent was to get at meanings, feelings, expectations, disappointments, and other symbolic behavior and its accompanying sentiments.

The remaining interviews may be roughly divided into two categories, one pertaining to different population groups and the other to television content. Of the first type, we designed interview schedules to be used with three different population groups: children aged six through seventeen (27 interviews), parents of young children (27 interviews), and people aged fifty through seventy (25 interviews). Our reason for designing schedules especially suited to these individual groups was that it was becoming increasingly clear that several of the central meanings and attractions of television could best be found by specific interviews of children, parents, and older people. While our regular interviewing would include some of these, it was thought desirable to prepare special sets of questions for each group.

The children's guide focused on their activities at home, school, and play; it asked about their parents and their siblings. It concentrated on their viewing habits, their favorite programs, the programs they don't like and those they can't watch, and in all instances their reasons for acting in or feeling a particular way. Their perception of their parents' attitudes toward television, specifically probed in these interviews, proved especially useful, for with the curiosity and candor of children they were often able to point directly, if innocently, to many of the central issues associated with TV viewing. Finally, the children's schedule asked about the television behavior of their friends, it sought to place this behavior and its value within the child's society, and it questioned these young respondents about the content and form of their favorite programs, performers, and commercials. A projective picture was used, as well as forced-choice types of questions.

The parents' interview guide began with general questions about the family and the children, what they are like and what they do on a "typical" weekday and a "typical" weekend. These and other questions sought to get at the interpersonal dynamics of the particular family, so that we could then better assess the place of television in this unique configuration of parents and children. We asked specifically, "What would you say are the most important influences in the lives of youngsters now growing up? Why?" and this information gave substantive information about their views on and uses of television, as well as opening up the topic of television in their home and its perceived and imagined effects on their children. Other questions dealt with the time spent by the children watching TV, the programs they watch regularly and occasionally, their favorite programs, and the reasons the parent believes they are favorites. Specific programs were singled out for discussion with the parent and his or her feelings about them in relation to the child. In a similar way, the parent was asked to comment on several commonly made statements, such as, "Television is a bad influence. Kids don't want to do their schoolwork and don't want to read any more," or "Television keeps kids busy and easier to manage." Incomplete sentence stems were used ("Bad manners...," "Television is...," "The cartoon programs..."), and a series of concluding questions pertained to the parent's own views of and behavior with television. With this information, we then could make more direct comparisons between the parent's attitudes and the ways in which he thought of the medium in relation to his children.

The schedule used with older people covered most of the same topics included in interview forms that were used with younger adult viewers, but with emphasis on getting at their perspective as elder citizens. They were asked about their uses of and feeling about television, what they consider the best thing about TV and the worst, which programs they know of and which they watch regularly, and why they use TV in this manner. We asked them to tell us how television fits their weekly routine, how on a certain evening they decide to watch a certain program, with whom they watch, the preferences of their spouse or other members of their household. In addition, the older men and women were asked to reflect on how television fits their present circumstances of life, how it has changed their living routine, how it affects other people, old and young alike. Finally, a series of questions that very specifically referred to their older age and its problems, all in relation to television, was asked. The interview schedule concluded with various projective and forced-choice questions.

The interview schedules related to television content were organized around commercials (three forms and a total of 75 interviews collected), personalities and performers (one form and 25 interviews), and programs (two forms and 50 interviews). These were used with adults of twenty to sixty years of age, and each was expected to provide fairly specific information about attitudes toward the program, performer, and commercial content of television. In designing and interpreting these interview schedules, we of course made use of what we had previously learned from the individual series of studies of these same matters.

One of the schedules oriented toward commercials focused on the relation between programs and commercials. It began by asking what programs are watched and then proceeded to probe about the commercials on these programs, what they are like and what they are for; whether the products advertised were ever purchased; if so, under what circumstances, and if not, why not; who might buy these advertised products, and so on. Comparisons between the commercials presented on different programs were then elicited, including direct comparisons of content and form, technique and mode of appeal, and the people who are thought to be most influenced by them. We attempted to get at purchase patterns in relation to television advertising and then obtained reactions to obviously negative statements about commercials. The respondent was asked about the "appropriate" kinds of products for different commercial forms (animated cartoons, commercials done by a comedy star, by the star of a musical-variety show or a Western, a commercial that explains how a product works, one that shows how to use a product, one that has singing and music, etc.). Questions on the proprieties of television advertising were included, some couched in terms of their effect on children. In conclusion, questions about the television advertising done by three different and familiar advertisers were asked, as well as questions about the sponsorship of six different performers then appearing on TV.

A second interview form on commercials attempted simply to examine commercials that stand out in the viewer's mind; it also sought to learn what were their main impressions of television advertising. The third form approached the same subject matter in relation to other forms of advertising (newspaper, magazines, radio) and from the perspective of the advertiser. It asked, for example, "What television program would you sponsor? Why? For this program, what sort of commercials would you use? Why?" It asked for opinions about different styles of advertising associated with different advertisers, and then the interviewer said, "Let's consider some specific commercials," probing for Coca-Cola, Chevrolet, Mr. Clean, headache-remedy commercials, cigarette commercials. The issues of the frequency of commercials and commercial interruptions were discussed, as was the possibility of commercials being "fixed."

The interview on television performers and personalities began by giving a long list of names to the respondent and asking for any and all thoughts and feelings about as many names on the list as he would like to comment on. We then probed for the viewer's ideas as to what makes for success and failure in this medium, for comparisons between being on television and being in movies, the theater, night clubs, and other forms of entertainment life. A question about the personal life of television entertainers was asked, as well as questions about TV writers, critics, and columnists, their relation to stars and their importance to viewers. Similar questions were asked about television producers, directors, and writers; about the popularity of some current stars; and several forced-choice questions having to do with television in general.

The interview schedules on programs were of two kinds. One, more oriented to television's content in general terms, included a series of open-ended questions on the values of TV, the people on television and their differing appeals, the quiz-program scandal, successful program formats, television violence, television appeals and problems, local versus national TV shows, the role of TV's critics, feelings about different networks, pay television, and new developments and innovations associated with the medium. The other schedule made use of actual program listings from local newspapers and

TV Guide. Going through the listing, the viewer was asked what he knew about the individual shows, which ones he watched and why, who appears on them, how he evaluates them, and so on. In all instances he was questioned about why he acts or feels in this way. We thus obtained a detailed record of what the viewer actually watched (very often much more than he himself thought he watched), as well as his evaluations of specific programs and their performers. The second half of the schedule shifted attention to television and its programs on a general level. It presented alternative ways of offering TV to the public (fewer hours of telecasting, for example) and then sought to determine what this would mean to the viewer and his family. It probed for views about TV spectaculars and about summer programing, and finished by offering several forced-choice, alternative-word pairs from which the viewer was asked to make choices reflecting his views of a television fan.

With these, as with the initial interview results, the mode of analysis was not only to look at the explicit content of the respondent's views and beliefs but also to examine these materials in terms of who the respondent was and to assess the meanings and implications of what he was saying, omitting to say, exaggerating, distorting, and the like. The analysis was done by several research people working in close co-operation, each examining independently many of the same materials.

Some of the sample statistics for these various studies are summarized in the following two tables. As already indicated, Table 1 refers to the fifty-nine individual show studies. Table 2 presents the total figures for several different sample characteristics for each of the three main types of studies: the fifty-nine individual show studies, the seven personality and two pilot-film investigations, and the one general study of television.

TABLE 1

A Sample Description of the Specific Television Program Studies

	Dinah Shore "Chevy Show" (11) N	%	Non-Dinah Shore "Chevy Show" (11) N	%	Adventure Shows (7) N	%	Musical-Variety, Star Shows (6) N	%	Pat Boone "Chevy Showroom" (5) N	%	Non-Chevrolet-Sponsored Musical-Variety Shows (5) N	%	Westerns (5) N	%	Current Events (3) N	%	Dramas (3) N	%	Mystery Shows (2) N	%	Situation Comedies (1) N	%	Total (59) N	%
SEX DISTRIBUTION																								
Men	1110	48	1081	48	683	49	624	50	480	48	424	49	524	50	262	47	306	49	190	48	103	48	5787	49
Women	1178	52	1144	51	715	51	635	50	520	52	440	50	528	50	291	53	310	50	210	52	110	52	6081	51
No response	3	*	4	*	—		—		6	*	6	1	1	—	—		7	1	—		—		27	*
Total	2291	100	2229	100	1398	100	1259	100	1006	100	870	100	1053	100	553	100	623	100	400	100	213	100	11,895	100
AGE DISTRIBUTION																								
18-30	335	15	306	14	265	19	217	17	196	19	125	14	211	20	98	18	106	17	78	20	39	18	1996	18
30-40	569	25	557	25	368	26	339	27	280	28	179	21	259	24	137	25	133	21	103	25	82	39	3006	24
40-50	527	23	485	22	326	23	278	22	213	21	172	20	218	21	123	22	145	24	93	23	40	19	2620	22
50-60	413	18	431	19	246	18	216	16	159	16	178	20	187	18	88	16	121	19	72	18	23	13	2134	18
60 and over	396	17	439	20	171	12	197	16	148	15	210	24	169	16	100	18	116	19	54	14	28	13	2028	17
No response	31	2	11	*	22	2	12	1	10	1	6	1	9	1	7	1	2	*	—		1	*	111	1
Total	2291	100	2229	100	1398	100	1259	100	1006	100	870	100	1053	100	553	100	623	100	400	100	213	100	11,895	100
SOCIAL-CLASS DISTRIBUTION																								
Upper middle class	303	13	262	11	149	11	188	15	83	8	97	11	79	7	108	20	115	18	57	14	16	8	1457	12
Lower middle class	1050	47	992	45	600	43	588	46	416	41	373	43	387	37	258	46	278	45	208	52	95	45	5245	44
Lower class	924	40	960	43	637	45	463	37	498	50	386	44	577	55	183	33	228	37	135	34	100	46	5091	43
No response	14	1	15	1	12	1	20	2	9	1	14	2	10	1	4	1	2	*	—		2	1	102	1
Total	2291	100	2229	100	1398	100	1259	100	1006	100	870	100	1053	100	553	100	623	100	400	100	213	100	11,895	100

T A B L E 1 – Continued

	Dinah Shore "Chevy Show" (11)	Non-Dinah Shore "Chevy Show" (11)	Adventure Shows (7)	Musical-Variety, Star Shows (6)	Pat Boone "Chevy Showroom" (5)	Non-Chevrolet-Sponsored Musical-Variety Shows (5)	Westerns (5)	Current Events (3)	Dramas (3)	Mystery Shows (2)	Situation Comedies (1)	Total (59)
CITY DISTRIBUTION†												
NORTHEAST REGION	432 (19)	397 (18)	246 (18)	234 (19)	194 (19)	171 (20)	176 (17)	134 (24)	127 (20)	79 (20)	37 (17)	2227 (19)
New York	95	41	122	121	114	49	—	—	—	—	—	542
Philadelphia	337	356	69	79	80	122	176	82	127	79	37	1544
Syracuse	—	—	55	34	—	—	—	52	—	—	—	141
SOUTHERN REGION	515 (22)	501 (22)	294 (21)	262 (21)	191 (19)	172 (20)	257 (24)	100 (18)	121 (20)	107 (27)	55 (27)	2575 (22)
Atlanta	408	434	160	193	191	172	109	41	121	77	26	1932
Oklahoma City	85	67	68	32	—	—	103	59	—	30	29	473
Dallas	22	—	66	37	—	—	45	—	—	—	—	170
EAST-CENTRAL REGION	98 (4)	67 (3)	176 (13)	77 (6)	—	—	118 (11)	64 (12)	—	—	37 (17)	637 (5)
Cincinnati	98	67	69	34	—	—	78	64	—	—	37	447
Louisville	—	—	107	43	—	—	40	—	—	—	—	190
WEST-CENTRAL REGION	802 (36)	864 (39)	415 (39)	421 (33)	420 (42)	359 (41)	329 (32)	215 (39)	251 (40)	144 (35)	47 (22)	4267 (36)
Chicago	372	411	219	221	209	180	177	113	125	67	10	2104
Denver	430	453	196	200	211	179	152	102	126	77	37	2163
WESTERN REGION	444 (19)	400 (18)	267 (19)	265 (21)	201 (20)	168 (19)	173 (16)	40 (7)	124 (20)	70 (18)	37 (17)	2189 (18)
Phoenix	22	—	69	35	—	—	35	—	—	—	—	161
Los Angeles	—	—	20	—	—	—	—	—	—	—	—	20
Portland	422	400	152	196	201	168	101	40	124	70	37	1,911
Seattle	—	—	26	34	—	—	37	—	—	—	—	97
GRAND TOTAL	2291 (100)	2229 (100)	1398 (100)	1259 (100)	1006 (100)	870 (100)	1053 (100)	553 (100)	623 (100)	400 (100)	213 (100)	11,895 (100)
SHOW EVALUATION												
Excellent	468 (20)	445 (20)	256 (18)	366 (29)	97 (10)	176 (20)	252 (24)	106 (19)	97 (16)	49 (12)	57 (27)	2369 (20)
Very good	853 (38)	785 (34)	572 (42)	444 (35)	327 (33)	305 (35)	403 (38)	148 (27)	129 (21)	116 (28)	106 (50)	4188 (34)
Good	509 (22)	443 (20)	263 (19)	243 (19)	222 (22)	197 (22)	266 (25)	68 (13)	65 (10)	84 (21)	40 (19)	2400 (20)
Fair	261 (11)	190 (9)	75 (5)	133 (11)	98 (10)	60 (7)	67 (6)	24 (4)	39 (6)	60 (15)	9 (4)	1016 (9)
Poor	56 (2)	84 (4)	20 (1)	40 (3)	22 (2)	20 (2)	6 (1)	5 (1)	19 (3)	27 (7)	1 (*)	299 (3)
Not asked/no response	144 (6)	282 (13)	212 (15)	33 (3)	240 (24)	112 (13)	59 (6)	202 (36)	274 (44)	64 (16)	*	1623 (14)
Total	2291 (100)	2229 (100)	1398 (100)	1259 (100)	1006 (100)	870 (100)	1053 (100)	553 (100)	623 (100)	400 (100)	213 (100)	11,895 (100)

* Less than one-half of 1 per cent.

† In each study one or more cities from each of the five Nielsen Television Index Geographic Territories was used for interviewing.

TABLE 2

A SAMPLE DESCRIPTION OF THREE TYPES OF TELEVISION STUDIES

	Specific Television-Program Studies (N=59)		TV Personality & Pilot-Film Studies (N=9)		General TV Study, 1960 (N=1)		Total Studies (N=69)	
	N	%						
Sex distribution								
Men	5,787	49	676	51	125	49	6,588	49
Women	6,081	51	644	48	130	51	6,855	51
No response	27	*	9	1	—	*	36	*
Total	11,895	100	1,329	100	255	100	13,479	100
Age distribution								
To 30 years	1,996	18	405	31	64	25	2,465	18
30 - 39 years	3,006	24	286	22	68	27	3,360	25
40 - 59 years	2,620	22	322	24	71	28	3,013	22
50 - 59 years	2,134	18	217	16	31	12	2,382	18
60 and over	2,028	17	84	6	20	8	2,132	16
No response	111	1	15	1	1	*	127	1
Total	11,895	100	1,329	100	255	100	13,479	100
Social-class distribution								
Upper middle class	1,457	12	201	15	50	20	1,708	13
Lower middle class	5,245	44	582	44	111	43	5,938	44
Lower class	5,091	43	545	41	94	37	5,730	42
No response	102	1	1	*	—	—	103	1
Total	11,895	100	1,329	100	255	100	13,479	100
City Distribution†								
Northeast region	2,227	19	202	15	54	21	2,483	18
New York	542		91		54		633	
Philadelphia	1,544		111		34		1,689	
Syracuse	141		—		—		141	
Worcester	—		—		20		20	

250

TABLE 2 — Continued

	Specific Television-Program Studies (N=59)		TV Personality & Pilot-Film Studies (N=9)		General TV Study, 1960 (N=1)		Total Studies (N=69)	
Southern region	2,575	22	231	17	41	16	2,847	21
Atlanta	1,932		231		25		2,188	
Oklahoma City	473		—		16		489	
Dallas	170		—		—		170	
East-central region	637	5	—	—	39	15	676	5
Cincinnati	447		—		26		473	
Louisville	190		—		13		203	
West-central region	4,267	36	695	53	95	38	5,057	38
Chicago	2,104		468		53		2,625	
Denver	2,163		227		—		2,390	
Mason City	—		—		42		42	
Western-region	2,189	18	201	15	26	10	2,416	18
Phoenix	161		—		—		161	
Los Angeles	20		—		—		20	
Portland	1,911		201		—		2,112	
Seattle	97		—		—		97	
San Francisco	—		—		26		26	
Grand Total	11,895	100	1,329	100	255	100	13,479	100
Show Evaluation								
Excellent	2,369	20	77	6	—	—	2,446	18
Very good	4,188	34	165	12	—	—	4,353	33
Good	2,400	20	122	9	—	—	2,522	19
Fair	1,016	9	60	5	—	—	1,076	8
Poor	299	3	20	3	—	—	319	2
Not asked/no response	1,623	14	885	65	255	100	2,763	20
Total	11,895	100	1,329	100	255	100	13,479	100

* Less than one-half of 1 per cent.

† In each study one or more cities from each of the five Nielsen Television Index Geographic Territories was used for interviewing.

ACKNOWLEDGMENTS

A book that derives from many research documents that have been prepared over an extended period of time has many authors. The two senior authors are responsible for the final version of this volume, but all five people listed on the title page were associated with the general study of television from which the book borrows in form and content. All were also involved in the individual program and personality studies, under the direction of Ira O. Glick and Edith Arlen; in addition, several other Social Research, Inc., staff members participated in these projects. Our appreciation for their thoughts, and in some instances for their words, is extended to our colleagues Dr. Barbara Berger, Dr. Eva F. Blatt, Dr. Richard P. Coleman, Gerald Handel, Douglas L. Hink, Bobette Adler Levy, Earl L. Kahn, Florence Mayer, Dr. Marc J. Swartz, Dr. Lee Rainwater, Carl S. Werthman, and, a consultant to Social Research, Inc., Professor Martin B. Loeb. Mrs. Levy also prepared the Index.

Mrs. Hope Roman was responsible for the statistical tabulations used extensively in the original research documents, and Dr. Benjamin D. Wright, one of the organization's consultants, aided in the development of statistical procedures that were incorporated in these studies.

The collection of interviews was under the direction of Mrs. Leone W. Phillips and her assistants, Mrs. Hanna Bratman and Miss Cynthia Fennander; their assistance is gratefully acknowledged. At various phases of the different studies, Dr. Burleigh B. Gardner, Executive Director of Social Research, Inc., contributed important ideas and concepts to the research. Professor W. Lloyd Warner, Senior Consultant at Social Research, Inc., was an active participant in many of the studies, and especially in the general television study; his understanding of the contemporary and emerging American social scene and his knowledge of the American social-class and symbol systems proved particularly helpful.

For over five years, Social Research, Inc., has enjoyed a close and stimulating relationship with Campbell-Ewald Company and several of its members. The authors appreciate the fact that the company agreed to our using the many studies undertaken in their behalf in the preparation of this volume. All responsibility for its content is, of course, that of the authors and not of Campbell-Ewald. John E. Bowen III, Assistant to the Vice-President, Marketing and Research Department, had direct responsibility for working with Social Research, Inc., during much of this time. His thinking and his efforts continuously made an important contribution to the various studies. In large measure the idea for the general television study carried out in 1960 was his; he offered many thoughts that were helpful to the authors in their conception of the project and that were incorporated into the research design. Throughout, he was a valuable and patient critic of our work and of the completed research document. It was under his instigation particularly that we were encouraged to prepare this manuscript for publication. For these things, and for the pleasant moments we have had working together with him, the authors wish to express their appreciation.

A number of other people at Campbell-Ewald Company also were associated with these studies. Mr. Philip L. McHugh, former Vice-President and Director of Television and Radio, ultimately received the results of these studies and put them to use. His probing questions often gave direction to our efforts. Mr. Peter S. Hoffman, former Assistant to the Vice-President and Director of Television and Radio, worked in much the same capacity. Miss Laura Baker, Research Account Executive, often had the task of reviewing our research reports and seeing that they were methodologically and interpretatively sound. Her efforts aided us in developing improved research devices and reporting techniques. To all these we express our gratitude.

INDEX

Accommodating stance: adult lower-middle class, 100-106; ambivalence in, 97-99; defined, 92; discussed, 92-106; main group of accommodators, summary of accommodators, 107-8.

Adams, Edie, 143

Adolescents: as protesters, 86-88; functions of TV for, 87-88; teen-age alienation, 86.

Adventure shows as program types, 131-33; attitudes about commercial appropriateness, 200

Adventures in Paradise, 49, 102, 132

Advertising worth of shows, 37-38; patterns of response to advertising, 204-28. See also Chapter 8, on commercials.

Alas Babylon, 53

Alcoa Presents, 218, 219

Aldred, Joel, 189; and Chevrolet, 190-91

Alfred Hitchcock Presents, 125

Alice in Wonderland, 53

Allen, Gracie, 143

Allen, Steve, 230

Allyson, June, 143

American Institute of Public Opinion (Gallup Poll), 75

Arnaz, Desi, 143, 163, 164

Arness, James, 62, 166

Arthur Murray Party, The, 130

Aspirin commercials, 176; Buferin and Dristan, 188

Astaire, Fred, 121, 145, 155, 230

At Random, 29, 131

Audience and attitude diversity, 19; "average audience," 22; core audience for each show, 38; descriptive differences, 19; differences in needs, 20-23; inadequacy of unitary concept, 42-43; summary of relationships, stances of embracers, protesters, accommodators, 106-8 (social class differences discussed in each section).

255

For Product Safety Concerns and Information please contact our EU
representative GPSR@taylorandfrancis.com Taylor & Francis Verlag GmbH,
Kaufingerstraße 24, 80331 München, Germany

Batch number: 08153793

Printed by Printforce, the Netherlands